I0084659

Gene Sharp & Bruce Jenkins
Fighting Tyranny

Gene Sharp & Bruce Jenkins

Fighting Tyranny

From Dictatorship to Democracy

and

The Anti-Coup

Spinebill Press

© Spinebill Press 2021

Text reproduced with permission
of the Albert Einstein Institution
aeinstein.org

All rights reserved. Apart from any fair dealing for
the purposes of private study, research, criticism or
review permitted under the Australian Copyright
Act 1968, no part may be stored or reproduced by any
process without prior permission. Enquiries should
be made to the publisher.

Spinebill Press
Katoomba NSW, Australia
spinebillpress.com

A catalogue record for this
book is available from the
National Library of Australia

NATIONAL
LIBRARY
OF AUSTRALIA

ISBN 978-0-6485315-1-7

Design and typography by Michel Streich
Typeset in Caslon and Myriad

Contents

Book One – **From Dictatorship to Democracy**

Book Two – The Anti-Coup

Appendices

From Dictatorship to Democracy

The Anti-Coup

Book One

From Dictatorship to Democracy
A Conceptual Framework for Liberation

by Gene Sharp

Preface

One of my major concerns for many years has been how people could prevent and destroy dictatorships. This has been nurtured in part because of a belief that human beings should not be dominated and destroyed by such regimes. That belief has been strengthened by readings on the importance of human freedom, on the nature of dictatorships (from Aristotle to analysts of totalitarianism), and histories of dictatorships (especially the Nazi and Stalinist systems).

Over the years I have had occasion to get to know people who lived and suffered under Nazi rule, including some who survived concentration camps. In Norway I met people who had resisted fascist rule and survived, and heard of those who perished. I talked with Jews who had escaped the Nazi clutches and with persons who had helped to save them.

Knowledge of the terror of Communist rule in various countries has been learned more from books than personal contacts. The terror of these systems appeared to me to be especially poignant for these dictatorships were imposed in the name of liberation from oppression and exploitation.

In more recent decades through visits of persons from dictatorially ruled countries, such as Panama, Poland, Chile, Tibet, and Burma, the realities of today's dictatorships became more real. From Tibetans who had fought against Chinese Communist aggression, Russians who had defeated the August 1991 hard-line coup, and Thais who had nonviolently blocked a return to military rule, I have gained often troubling perspectives on the insidious nature of dictatorships.

The sense of pathos and outrage against the brutalities, along with admiration of the calm heroism of unbelievably brave men and women, were sometimes strengthened by visits to places where the dangers were still great, and yet defiance by brave people continued. These included Panama under Noriega; Vilnius, Lithuania, under continued Soviet repression; Tiananmen Square, Beijing, during both the festive demonstration of freedom and while the first armoured personnel carriers entered that fateful night; and the jungle headquarters of the democratic opposition at Manerplaw in "liberated Burma."

Sometimes I visited the sites of the fallen, as the television tower and the cemetery in Vilnius, the public park in Riga where people had been gunned down, the centre of Ferrara in northern Italy where the fascists lined up and shot resisters, and a simple cemetery in Manerplaw filled with bodies of men who had died much too young. It is a sad realisation that every dictatorship leaves such death and destruction in its wake.

Out of these concerns and experiences grew a de-termined hope that prevention of tyranny might be possible, that successful struggles against dictatorships could be waged without mass mutual slaughters, that dictatorships could be destroyed and new ones prevented from rising out of the ashes.

I have tried to think carefully about the most effective ways in which dictatorships could be successfully disintegrated with the least possible cost in suffering and lives. In this I have drawn on my studies over many years of dictatorships, resistance movements, revolutions, political thought, governmental systems, and especially realistic nonviolent struggle.

This publication is the result. I am certain it is far from perfect. But, perhaps, it offers some guidelines to assist thought and planning to produce movements of liberation that are more powerful and effective than might otherwise be the case.

Of necessity, and of deliberate choice, the focus of this essay is on the generic problem of how to destroy a dictatorship and to prevent the rise of a new one. I am not competent to produce a detailed analysis and prescription for a particular country. However, it is my hope that this generic analysis may be useful to people in, unfortunately, too many countries who now face the realities of dictatorial rule. They will need to examine the validity of this analysis for their situations and the extent to which its major recommendations are, or can be made to be, applicable for their liberation struggles.

Nowhere in this analysis do I assume that defying dictators will be an easy or cost-free endeavour. All forms of struggle have complications and costs. Fighting dictators will, of course, bring casualties. It is my hope, however, that this analysis will spur resistance leaders to consider strategies that may increase their effective power while reducing the relative level of casualties.

Nor should this analysis be interpreted to mean that when a specific dictatorship is ended, all other problems will also disappear. The fall of one regime does not bring in a utopia. Rather, it opens the way for hard work and long efforts to build more just social, economic, and political relationships and the eradication of other forms of injustices and oppression. It is my hope that this brief examination of how a dictatorship can be disintegrated may be found useful wherever people live under domination and desire to be free.

6 OCTOBER 1993
ALBERT EINSTEIN INSTITUTION
BOSTON, MASSACHUSETTS

One

Facing Dictatorships Realistically

In recent years various dictatorships – of both internal and external origin – have collapsed or stumbled when confronted by defiant, mobilised people. Often seen as firmly entrenched and impregnable, some of these dictatorships proved unable to withstand the concerted political, economic, and social defiance of the people.

Since 1980 dictatorships have collapsed before the predominantly nonviolent defiance of people in Estonia, Latvia, and Lithuania, Poland, East Germany, Czechoslovakia and Slovenia, Madagascar, Mali, Bolivia, and the Philippines. Nonviolent resistance has furthered the movement toward democratisation in Nepal, Zambia, South Korea, Chile, Argentina, Haiti, Brazil, Uruguay, Malawi, Thailand, Bulgaria, Hungary, Nigeria, and various parts of the former Soviet Union (playing a significant role in the defeat of the August 1991 attempted hard-line coup d'état).

In addition, mass political defiance[1] has occurred in China, Burma, and Tibet in recent years. Although those struggles have not brought an end to the ruling dictatorships or occupations, they have exposed the brutal nature of those repressive regimes to the world community and have provided the populations with valuable experience with this form of struggle.

The collapse of dictatorships in the above named

countries certainly has not erased all other problems in those societies: poverty, crime, bureaucratic inefficiency, and environmental destruction are often the legacy of brutal regimes. However, the downfall of these dictatorships has minimally lifted much of the suffering of the victims of oppression, and has opened the way for the rebuilding of these societies with greater political democracy, personal liberties, and social justice.

A continuing problem

There has indeed been a trend towards greater democratisation and freedom in the world in the past decades. According to Freedom House, which compiles a yearly international survey of the status of political rights and civil liberties, the number of countries around the world classified as "Free" has grown significantly in recent years[2]:

	Free	partly Free	not Free
1983	54	47	64
1993	75	73	38
2003	89	55	48
2009	89	62	42

However, this positive trend is tempered by the large numbers of people still living under conditions of tyranny. As of 2008, 34% of the world's 6.68 billion population lived in countries designated as "Not Free,"[3] that is, areas with extremely restricted political rights and civil liberties. The 42 countries in the "Not Free" category are ruled by a range of military dictatorships (as in Burma), traditional repressive monarchies (as in Saudi Arabia and Bhutan), dominant political parties (as in China and North Korea), foreign occupiers (as in Tibet and Western Sahara), or are in a state of transition.

Many countries today are in a state of rapid economic, political, and social change. Although the number of "Free" countries has increased in recent years, there is a great risk that many nations, in the face of such rapid fundamental changes, will move in the opposite direction and experience new forms of dictatorship. Military cliques, ambitious individuals, elected officials, and doctrinal political parties will repeatedly seek to impose their will. *Coups d'état* are and will remain a common occurrence. Basic human and political rights will continue to be denied to vast numbers of peoples.

Unfortunately, the past is still with us. The problem of dictatorships is deep. People in many countries have experienced decades or even centuries of oppression, whether of domestic or foreign origin. Frequently, unquestioning submission to authority figures and rulers has been long inculcated. In extreme cases, the social, political, economic, and even religious in-stitutions of the society – outside of state control – have been deliberately weakened, subordinated, or even replaced by new regimented institutions used by the state or ruling party to control the society.

The population has often been atomised (turned into a mass of isolated individuals) unable to work together to achieve freedom, to confide in each other, or even to do much of anything at their own initiative.

The result is predictable: the population becomes weak, lacks self-confidence, and is incapable of resistance. People are often too frightened to share their hatred of the dictatorship and their hunger for freedom even with family and friends. People are often too terrified to think seriously of public resistance. In any case, what would be the use? Instead, they face suffering without purpose and a future without hope.

Current conditions in today's dictatorships may be much worse than earlier. In the past, some people may have attempted resistance. Short-lived mass protests and demonstrations may have occurred. Perhaps spirits soared temporarily. At other times, individuals and small groups may have conducted brave but impotent gestures, asserting some principle or simply their defiance. However noble the motives, such past acts of resistance have often been insufficient to overcome the people's fear and habit of obedience, a necessary prerequisite to destroy the dictatorship. Sadly, those acts may have brought instead only increased suffering and death, not victories or even hope.

Freedom through violence?

What is to be done in such circumstances? The obvious possibilities seem useless. Constitutional and legal barriers, judicial decisions, and public opinion are normally ignored by dictators. Understandably, reacting to the brutalities, torture, disappearances, and killings, people often have concluded that only violence can end a dictatorship. Angry victims have sometimes organised to fight the brutal dictators with whatever violent and military capacity they could muster, despite the odds being against them. These people have often fought bravely, at great cost in suffering and lives. Their accomplishments have sometimes been remarkable, but they rarely have won freedom. Violent rebellions can trigger brutal repression that frequently leaves the populace more helpless than before.

Whatever the merits of the violent option, however, one point is clear. *By placing confidence in violent means, one has chosen the very type of struggle with which the oppressors nearly always have superiority.* The dictators are equipped to apply violence overwhelmingly. However long or briefly these democrats can continue, eventually the harsh military realities usually become inescapable. The dictators almost always have superiority in military hardware, ammunition, transportation, and the size of military forces. Despite bravery, the democrats are (almost always) no match.

When conventional military rebellion is recognised as unrealistic, some dissidents then favour guerrilla warfare. However, guerrilla warfare rarely, if ever, benefits the oppressed population or ushers in a democracy. Guerrilla warfare is no obvious solution, particularly given the very strong tendency toward immense casualties among one's own people. The technique is no guarantor against failure, despite supporting theory and strategic analyses, and sometimes international backing. Guerrilla struggles often last a very long time. Civilian populations are often displaced by the ruling government, with immense human suffering and social dislocation. Even when successful, guerrilla struggles often have significant long-term negative structural consequences. Immediately, the attacked regime becomes more dictatorial as a result of its countermeasures. If the guerrillas should finally succeed, the resulting new regime is often more dictatorial than its predecessor due to the centralising impact of the expanded military forces and the weakening or destruction of the society's independent groups and institutions during the struggle – bodies that are vital in establishing and maintaining a democratic society. Persons hostile to dictatorships should look for another option.

Coups, elections, foreign saviors?

A military coup d'état against a dictatorship might appear to be relatively one of the easiest and quickest ways to remove a particularly repugnant regime.

However, there are very serious problems with that technique. Most importantly, it leaves in place the existing maldistribution of power between the population and the elite in control of the government and its military forces. The removal of particular persons and cliques from the governing positions most likely will merely make it possible for another group to take their place. Theoretically, this group might be milder in its behavior and be open in limited ways to democratic reforms. However, the opposite is as likely to be the case.

After consolidating its position, the new clique may turn out to be more ruthless and more ambitious than the old one. Consequently, the new clique – in which hopes may have been placed – will be able to do whatever it wants without concern for democracy or human rights. That is not an acceptable answer to the problem of dictatorship.

Elections are not available under dictatorships as an instrument of significant political change. Some dictatorial regimes, such as those of the former Soviet-dominated Eastern bloc, went through the motions in order to appear democratic. Those elections, however, were merely rigidly controlled plebiscites to get public endorsement of candidates already hand picked by the dictators. Dictators under pressure may at times agree to new elections, but then rig them to place civilian puppets in government offices. If opposition candidates have been allowed to run and were actually elected, as occurred in Burma in 1990 and Nigeria in 1993, results may simply be ignored and the "victors" subjected to intimidation, arrest, or even execution. Dictators are not in the business of allowing elections that could remove them from their thrones.

Many people now suffering under a brutal dictatorship, or who have gone into exile to escape its immediate grasp, do not believe that the oppressed can liberate themselves. They expect that their people can only be saved by the actions of others. These people place their confidence in external forces. They believe that only international help can be strong enough to bring down the dictators.

The view that the oppressed are unable to act effectively is sometimes accurate for a certain time period. As noted, often oppressed people are unwilling and temporarily unable to struggle because they have no confidence in their ability to face the ruthless dictatorship, and no known way to save themselves. It is therefore understandable that many people place their hope for liberation in others. This outside force may be "public opinion," the United Nations, a particular country, or international economic and political sanctions.

Such a scenario may sound comforting, but there are grave problems with this reliance on an outside savior. Such confidence may be totally misplaced. Usually no foreign saviors are coming, and if a foreign state does intervene, it probably should not be trusted.

A few harsh realities concerning reliance on foreign intervention need to be emphasised here:

• Frequently foreign states will tolerate, or even positively assist, a dictatorship in order to advance their own economic or political interests.

• Foreign states also may be willing to sell out an oppressed people instead of keeping pledges to assist their liberation at the cost of another objective.

• Some foreign states will act against a dictatorship only to gain their own economic, political, or military control over the country.

• The foreign states may become actively involved for positive purposes only if and when the internal resistance movement has already begun shaking the dictatorship, having thereby focused international attention on the brutal nature of the regime.

Dictatorships usually exist primarily because of the internal power distribution in the home country. The population and society are too weak to cause the dictatorship serious problems, wealth and power are concentrated in too few hands. Although dictatorships may benefit from or be somewhat weakened by international actions, their continuation is dependent primarily on internal factors.

International pressures can be very useful, however, when they are supporting a powerful internal resistance movement. Then, for example, international economic boycotts, embargoes, the breaking of diplomatic relations, expulsion from international organisations, condemnation by United Nations bodies, and the like can assist greatly. However, in the absence of a strong internal resistance movement such actions by others are unlikely to happen.

Facing the hard truth

The conclusion is a hard one. When one wants to bring down a dictatorship most effectively and with the least cost then one has four immediate tasks:

• One must strengthen the oppressed population themselves in their determination, self-confidence, and resistance skills;

• One must strengthen the independent social groups and institutions of the oppressed people;

• One must create a powerful internal resistance force; and

• One must develop a wise grand strategic plan for liberation and implement it skillfully.

A liberation struggle is a time for self-reliance and internal strengthening of the struggle group. As Charles Stewart Parnell called out during the Irish rent strike campaign in 1879 and 1880:

It is no use relying on the Government . . . . You must only rely upon your own determination. ... [H]elp yourselves by standing together ... strengthen those amongst yourselves who are weak ..., band yourselves together, organise yourselves ... and you must win ...

When you have made this question ripe for settlement, then and not till then will it be settled.[4]

Against a strong self-reliant force, given wise strategy, disciplined and courageous action, and genuine strength, the dictatorship will eventually crumble. Minimally, however, the above four requirements must be fulfilled.

As the above discussion indicates, liberation from dictatorships ultimately depends on the people's ability to liberate themselves. The cases of successful political defiance – or nonviolent struggle for political ends – cited above indicate that the means do exist for populations to free themselves, but that option has remained undeveloped. We will examine this option in detail in the following chapters. However, we should first look at the issue of negotiations as a means of dismantling dictatorships.

Two

The Dangers of Negotiations

When faced with the severe problems of confronting a dictatorship (as surveyed in Chapter One), some people may lapse back into passive submission. Others, seeing no prospect of achieving democracy, may conclude they must come to terms with the apparently permanent dictatorship, hoping that through "conciliation," "compromise," and "negotiations" they might be able to salvage some positive elements and to end the brutalities. On the surface, lacking realistic options, there is appeal in that line of thinking.

Serious struggle against brutal dictatorships is not a pleasant prospect. Why is it necessary to go that route? Can't everyone just be reasonable and find ways to talk, to negotiate the way to a gradual end to the dictatorship? Can't the democrats appeal to the dictators' sense of common humanity and convince them to reduce their domination bit by bit, and perhaps finally to give way completely to the establishment of a democracy?

It is sometimes argued that the truth is not all on one side. Perhaps the democrats have misunderstood the dictators, who may have acted from good motives in difficult circumstances? Or perhaps some may think, the dictators would gladly remove themselves from the difficult situation facing the country if only given some encouragement and enticements. It may be argued that the dictators could be offered a "win-win" solution, in which everyone gains something. The risks and pain of further struggle could be unnecessary, it may be argued, if the democratic opposition is only willing to settle the conflict peacefully by negotiations (which may even perhaps be assisted by some skilled individuals or even another government). Would that not be preferable to a difficult struggle, even if it is one conducted by nonviolent struggle rather than by military war?

Merits and limitations of negotiations

Negotiations are a very useful tool in resolving certain types of issues in conflicts and should not be neglected or rejected when they are appropriate.

In some situations where no fundamental issues are at stake, and therefore a compromise is acceptable, negotiations can be an important means to settle a conflict. A labour strike for higher wages is a good example of the appropriate role of negotiations in a conflict: a negotiated settlement may provide an increase somewhere between the sums originally proposed by each of the contending sides. Labour conflicts with legal trade unions are, however, quite different than the conflicts in which the continued existence of a cruel dictatorship or the establishment of political freedom are at stake.

When the issues at stake are fundamental, affecting

religious principles, issues of human freedom, or the whole future development of the society, negotiations do not provide a way of reaching a mutually satisfactory solution. On some basic issues there should be no compromise. Only a shift in power relations in favour of the democrats can adequately safeguard the basic issues at stake. Such a shift will occur through struggle, not negotiations. This is not to say that negotiations ought never to be used. The point here is that negotiations are not a realistic way to remove a strong dictatorship in the absence of a powerful democratic opposition.

Negotiations, of course, may not be an option at all. Firmly entrenched dictators who feel secure in their position may refuse to negotiate with their democratic opponents. Or, when negotiations have been initiated, the democratic negotiators may disappear and never be heard from again.

Negotiated surrender?

Individuals and groups who oppose dictatorship and favour negotiations will often have good motives. Especially when a military struggle has continued for years against a brutal dictatorship without final victory, it is understandable that all the people of whatever political persuasion would want peace. Negotiations are especially likely to become an issue among democrats where the dictators have clear military superiority and the destruction and casualties among one's own people are no longer bearable. There will then be a strong temptation to explore any other route that might salvage some of the democrats' objectives while bringing an end to the cycle of violence and counter-violence.

The offer by a dictatorship of "peace" through negotiations with the democratic opposition is, of course, rather disingenuous. The violence could be ended immediately by the dictators themselves, if only they would stop waging war on their own people. They could at their own initiative without any bargaining restore respect for human dignity and rights, free political prisoners, end torture, halt military operations, withdraw from the government, and apologise to the people.

When the dictatorship is strong but an irritating resistance exists, the dictators may wish to negotiate the opposition into surrender under the guise of making "peace." The call to negotiate can sound appealing, but grave dangers can be lurking within the negotiating room.

On the other hand, when the opposition is exceptionally strong and the dictatorship is genuinely threatened, the dictators may seek negotiations in order to salvage as much of their control or wealth as possible. In neither case should the democrats help the dictators achieve their goals.

Democrats should be wary of the traps that may be deliberately built into a negotiation process by the dictators. The call for negotiations when basic issues of political liberties are involved may be an effort by the dictators to induce the democrats to surrender peacefully while the violence of the dictatorship continues. In those types of conflicts the only proper role of negotiations may occur at the end of a decisive struggle in which the power of the dictators has been effectively destroyed and they seek personal safe passage to an international airport.

Power and justice in negotiations

If this judgment sounds too harsh a commentary on negotiations, perhaps some of the romanticism associated with them needs to be moderated. Clear thinking is required as to how negotiations operate.

"Negotiation" does not mean that the two sides sit down together on a basis of equality and talk through and resolve the differences that produced the conflict between them. Two facts must be remembered. First, in negotiations it is not the relative justice of the conflicting views and objectives that determines the content of a negotiated agreement. Second, the content of a negotiated agreement is largely determined by the power capacity of each side.

Several difficult questions must be considered. What can each side do at a later date to gain its objectives if the other side fails to come to an agreement at the negotiating table? What can each side do after an agreement is reached if the other side breaks its word and uses its available forces to seize its objectives despite the agreement? A settlement is not reached in negotiations through an assessment of the rights and wrongs of the issues at stake. While those may be much discussed, the real results in negotiations come from an assessment of the absolute and relative power situations of the contending groups. What can the democrats do to ensure that their minimum claims cannot be denied? What can the dictators do to stay in control and neutralise the democrats? In other words, if an agreement comes, it is more likely the result of each side estimating how the power capacities of the two sides compare, and then calculating how an open struggle might end.

Attention must also be given to what each side is willing to give up in order to reach agreement. In successful negotiations there is compromise, a splitting of differences. Each side gets part of what it wants and gives up part of its objectives.

In the case of extreme dictatorships what are the pro-democracy forces to give up to the dictators? What objectives of the dictators are the pro-democracy forces to accept? Are the democrats to give to the dictators (whether a political party or a military cabal) a constitutionally-established permanent role in the future government? Where is the democracy in that?

Even assuming that all goes well in negotiations, it is necessary to ask: What kind of peace will be the result? Will life then be better or worse than it would be if the democrats began or continued to struggle?

Dictators may have a variety of motives and objectives underlying their domination: power, position, wealth, reshaping the society, and the like. One should remember that none of these will be served if they abandon their control positions. In the event of negotiations dictators will try to preserve their goals.

Whatever promises offered by dictators in any negotiated settlement, no one should ever forget that the dictators may promise anything to secure submission from their democratic opponents, and then brazenly violate those same agreements.

If the democrats agree to halt resistance in order to gain a reprieve from repression, they may be very disappointed. A halt to resistance rarely brings reduced repression. Once the restraining force of internal and international opposition has been removed, dictators may even make their oppression and violence more brutal than before. The collapse of popular resistance often removes the countervailing force that has limited the control and brutality of the dictatorship. The tyrants can then move ahead against whomever they wish. "For the tyrant has the power to inflict only that which we lack the strength to resist," wrote Krishnalal Shridharani.[5]

Resistance, not negotiations, is essential for change in conflicts where fundamental issues are at stake. In nearly all cases, resistance must continue to drive dictators out of power. Success is most often determined not by negotiating a settlement but through the wise use of the most appropriate and powerful means of resistance available. It is our contention, to be explored later in more detail, that political defiance, or nonviolent struggle, is the most powerful means available to those struggling for freedom.

What kind of peace?

If dictators and democrats are to talk about peace at all, extremely clear thinking is needed because of the dangers involved. Not everyone who uses the word "peace" wants peace with freedom and justice. Submission to cruel oppression and passive acquiescence to ruthless dictators who have perpetrated atrocities on hundreds of thousands of people is no real peace. Hitler often called for peace, by which he meant submission to his will. A dictators' peace is often no more than the peace of the prison or of the grave.

There are other dangers. Well-intended negotiators sometimes confuse the objectives of the negotiations and the negotiation process itself. Further, democratic negotiators, or foreign negotiation specialists accepted to assist in the negotiations, may in a single stroke provide the dictators with the domestic and international legitimacy that they had been previously denied because of their seizure of the state, human rights violations, and brutalities. Without that desperately needed legitimacy, the dictators cannot continue to rule indefinitely. Exponents of peace should not provide them legitimacy.

Reasons for hope

As stated earlier, opposition leaders may feel forced to pursue negotiations out of a sense of hopelessness of the democratic struggle. However, that sense of powerlessness can be changed. Dictatorships are not permanent. People living under dictatorships need not remain weak, and dictators need not be allowed to remain powerful indefinitely. Aristotle noted long ago, "... [O]ligarchy and tyranny are shorter-lived than any other constitution. ... [A]ll round, tyrannies have not lasted long."[6] Modern dictatorships are also vulnerable. Their weaknesses can be aggravated and the dictators' power can be disintegrated. (In Chapter Four we will examine these weaknesses in more detail.)

Recent history shows the vulnerability of dictatorships, and reveals that they can crumble in a relatively short time span: whereas ten years – 1980-1990 – were required to bring down the Communist dictatorship in Poland, in East Germany and Czechoslovakia in 1989 it occurred within weeks. In El Salvador and Guatemala in 1944 the struggles against the entrenched brutal military dictators required approximately two weeks each. The militarily powerful regime of the Shah in Iran was undermined in a few months. The Marcos dictatorship in the Philippines fell before people power within weeks in 1986: the United States government quickly abandoned President Marcos when the strength of the opposition became apparent. The attempted hard-line coup in the Soviet Union in August 1991 was blocked in days by political defiance. Thereafter, many of its long dominated constituent nations in only days, weeks, and months regained their independence.

The old preconception that violent means always work quickly and nonviolent means always require vast time is clearly not valid. Although much time may be required for changes in the underlying situation and society, the actual fight against a dictatorship sometimes occurs relatively quickly by nonviolent struggle.

Negotiations are not the only alternative to a continuing war of annihilation on the one hand and capitulation on the other. The examples just cited, as well as those listed in Chapter One, illustrate that another option exists for those who want both peace and freedom: political defiance.

Three

Whence Comes the Power?

Achieving a society with both freedom and peace is of course no simple task. It will require great strategic skill, organisation, and planning. Above all, it will require power. Democrats cannot hope to bring down a dictatorship and establish political freedom without the ability to apply their own power effectively.

But how is this possible? What kind of power can the democratic opposition mobilise that will be sufficient to destroy the dictatorship and its vast military and police networks? The answers lie in an oft ignored understanding of political power. Learning this insight is not really so difficult a task. Some basic truths are quite simple.

The "Monkey Master" fable

A fourteenth century Chinese parable by Liu-Ji, for example, outlines this neglected understanding of political power quite well:[7]

In the feudal state of Chu an old man survived by keeping monkeys in his service. The people of Chu called him "*ju gong*" (monkey master).

Each morning, the old man would assemble the monkeys in his courtyard, and order the eldest one to lead the others to the mountains to gather fruits from bushes and trees. It was the rule that each monkey had to give one-tenth of his collection to the old man. Those who failed to do so would be ruthlessly flogged. All the monkeys suffered bitterly, but dared not complain.

One day, a small monkey asked the other monkeys: "Did the old man plant all the fruit trees and bushes?" The others said: "No, they grew naturally." The small monkey further asked: "Can't we take the fruits without the old man's permission?" The others replied: "Yes, we all can." The small monkey continued: "Then, why should we depend on the old man; why must we all serve him?"

Before the small monkey was able to finish his statement, all the monkeys suddenly became en-lightened and awakened.

On the same night, watching that the old man had fallen asleep, the monkeys tore down all the barricades of the stockade in which they were confined, and destroyed the stockade entirely. They also took the fruits the old man had in storage, brought all with them to the woods, and never returned. The old man finally died of starvation.

Yu-li-zi says, "Some men in the world rule their people by tricks and not by righteous principles. Aren't they just like the monkey master? They are not aware of their muddle-headedness. As soon as their people become enlightened, their tricks no longer work."

The principle is simple. Dictators require the assistance of the people they rule, without which they cannot secure and maintain the sources of political power. These sources of political power include:

• *Authority*, the belief among the people that the regime is legitimate, and that they have a moral duty to obey it;

• *Human resources*, the number and importance of the persons and groups which are obeying, cooperating, or providing assistance to the rulers;

• *Skills and knowledge*, needed by the regime to perform specific actions and supplied by the cooperating persons and groups;

• *Intangible factors*, psychological and ideological factors that may induce people to obey and assist the rulers;

• *Material resources*, the degree to which the rulers control or have access to property, natural resources, financial resources, the economic system, and means of communication and transportation; and

• *Sanctions*, punishments, threatened or applied, against the disobedient and noncooperative to ensure the submission and cooperation that are needed for the regime to exist and carry out its policies.

All of these sources, however, depend on acceptance of the regime, on the submission and obedience of the population, and on the cooperation of innumerable people and the many institutions of the society. These are not guaranteed.

Full cooperation, obedience, and support will increase the availability of the needed sources of power and, consequently, expand the power capacity of any government.

On the other hand, withdrawal of popular and institutional cooperation with aggressors and dictators diminishes, and may sever, the availability of the sources of power on which all rulers depend. Without availability of those sources, the rulers' power weakens and finally dissolves.

Naturally, dictators are sensitive to actions and ideas that threaten their capacity to do as they like. Dictators are therefore likely to threaten and punish those who disobey, strike, or fail to cooperate. However, that is not the end of the story. Repression, even brutalities, do not always produce a resumption of the necessary degree of submission and cooperation for the regime to function.

If, despite repression, the sources of power can be restricted or severed for enough time, the initial results may be uncertainty and confusion within the dictatorship. That is likely to be followed by a clear weakening of the power of the dictatorship. Over time, the withholding of the sources of power can produce the paralysis and impotence of the regime, and in severe cases, its disintegration. The dictators' power will die, slowly or rapidly, from political starvation. The degree of liberty or tyranny in any government is, it follows, in large degree a reflection of the relative determination of the subjects to be free and their willingness and ability to resist efforts to enslave them.

Contrary to popular opinion, even totalitarian dictatorships are dependent on the population and the societies they rule. As the political scientist Karl W. Deutsch noted in 1953:

> *Totalitarian power is strong only if it does not have to be used too often. If totalitarian power must be used at all times against the entire population, it is unlikely to remain powerful for long. Since totalitarian regimes require more power for dealing with their subjects than do other types of government, such regimes stand in greater need of widespread and dependable compliance habits among their people; more than that they have to be able to count on the active support of at least significant parts of the population in case of need.*[8]

The English nineteenth century legal theorist John Austin described the situation of a dictatorship confronting a disaffected people. Austin argued that if most of the population were determined to destroy the government and were willing to endure repression to do so, then the might of the government, including those who supported it, could not preserve the hated government, even if it received foreign assistance. The defiant people could not be forced back into permanent obedience and subjection, Austin concluded.[9] Niccolo Machiavelli had much earlier argued that the prince "... who has the public as a whole for his enemy can never make himself secure; and the greater his cruelty, the weaker does his regime become."[10]

The practical political application of these insights was demonstrated by the heroic Norwegian resisters against the Nazi occupation, and as cited in Chapter One, by the brave Poles, Germans, Czechs, Slovaks, and many others who resisted Communist aggression and dictatorship, and finally helped produce the collapse of Communist rule in Europe. This, of course, is no new phenomenon: cases of nonviolent resistance go back at least to 494 B.C. when plebeians withdrew cooperation from their Roman patrician masters.[11] Nonviolent struggle has been employed at various times by peoples throughout Asia, Africa, the Americas, Australasia, and the Pacific islands, as well as Europe.

Three of the most important factors in determining to what degree a government's power will be controlled or uncontrolled therefore are: (1) the relative desire of the populace to impose limits on the government's power; (2) the relative strength of the subjects' independent organisations and institutions to withdraw collectively the sources of power; and (3) the population's relative ability to withhold their consent and assistance.

One characteristic of a democratic society is that there exist independent of the state a multitude of non-governmental groups and institutions. These include, for example, families, religious organisations, cultural associations, sports clubs, economic institutions, trade unions, student associations, political parties, villages, neighbourhood associations, gardening clubs, human rights organisations, musical groups, literary societies, and others. These bodies are important in serving their own objectives and also in helping to meet social needs.

Additionally, these bodies have great political significance. They provide group and institutional bases by which people can exert influence over the direction of their society and resist other groups or the government when they are seen to impinge unjustly on their interests, activities, or purposes. Isolated individuals, not members of such groups, usually are unable to make a significant impact on the rest of the society, much less a government, and certainly not a dictatorship.

Consequently, if the autonomy and freedom of such bodies can be taken away by the dictators, the population will be relatively helpless. Also, if these institutions can themselves be dictatorially controlled by the central regime or replaced by new controlled ones, they can be used to dominate both the individual members and also those areas of the society.

However, if the autonomy and freedom of these independent civil institutions (outside of government control) can be maintained or regained they are highly important for the application of political defiance. The common feature of the cited examples in which dictatorships have been disintegrated or weakened has been the courageous mass application of political defiance by the population and its institutions.

As stated, these centres of power provide the institutional bases from which the population can exert pressure or can resist dictatorial controls. In the future, they will be part of the indispensable structural base for a free society. Their continued independence and growth therefore is often a prerequisite for the success of the liberation struggle.

If the dictatorship has been largely successful in destroying or controlling the society's independent bodies, it will be important for the resisters to create new independent social groups and institutions, or to reassert democratic control over surviving or partially controlled bodies. During the Hungarian Revolution of 1956-1957 a multitude of direct democracy councils emerged, even joining together to establish for some weeks a whole federated system of institutions and governance. In Poland during the late 1980s workers maintained illegal Solidarity unions and, in some cases, took over control of the official, Communist-dominated, trade unions. Such institutional developments can have very important political consequences.

Of course, none of this means that weakening and destroying dictatorships is easy, nor that every attempt will succeed. It certainly does not mean that the struggle will be free of casualties, for those still serving the dictators are likely to fight back in an effort to force the populace to resume cooperation and obedience.

The above insight into power does mean, however, that the deliberate disintegration of dictatorships is possible. Dictatorships in particular have specific characteristics that render them highly vulnerable to skillfully implemented political defiance. Let us examine these characteristics in more detail.

Four

Dictatorships Have Weaknesses

Dictatorships often appear invulnerable. Intelligence agencies, police, military forces, prisons, concentration camps, and execution squads are controlled by a powerful few. A country's finances, natural resources, and production capacities are often arbitrarily plundered by dictators and used to support the dictators' will.

In comparison, democratic opposition forces often appear extremely weak, ineffective, and powerless. That perception of invulnerability against powerlessness makes effective opposition unlikely.

That is not the whole story, however.

Identifying the Achilles' heel

A myth from classical Greece illustrates well the vulnerability of the supposedly invulnerable. Against the warrior Achilles, no blow would injure and no sword would penetrate his skin. When still a baby, Achilles' mother had supposedly dipped him into the waters of the magical river Styx, resulting in the protection of his body from all dangers. There was, however, a problem. Since the baby was held by his heel so that he would not be washed away, the magical water had not covered that small part of his body. When Achilles was a grown man he appeared to all to be invulnerable to the enemies' weapons. However, in the battle against Troy, instructed by one who knew the weakness, an enemy soldier aimed his arrow at Achilles' unprotected heel, the one spot where he could be injured. The strike proved fatal. Still today, the phrase "Achilles' heel" refers to the vulnerable part of a person, a plan, or an institution at which if attacked there is no protection. The same principle applies to ruthless dictatorships. They, too, can be conquered, but most quickly and with least cost if their weaknesses can be identified and the attack concentrated on them.

Weaknesses of dictatorships

Among the weaknesses of dictatorships are the following:

1. The cooperation of a multitude of people, groups, and institutions needed to operate the system may be restricted or withdrawn.

2. The requirements and effects of the regime's past policies will somewhat limit its present ability to adopt and implement conflicting policies.

3. The system may become routine in its operation, less able to adjust quickly to new situations.

4. Personnel and resources already allocated for existing tasks will not be easily available for new needs.

5. Subordinates fearful of displeasing their superiors may not report accurate or complete information needed by the dictators to make decisions.

6. The ideology may erode, and myths and symbols of the system may become unstable.

7. If a strong ideology is present that influences one's view of reality, firm adherence to it may cause inattention to actual conditions and needs.

8. Deteriorating efficiency and competency of the bureaucracy, or excessive controls and regulations, may make the system's policies and operation ineffective.

9. Internal institutional conflicts and personal rivalries and hostilities may harm, and even disrupt, the operation of the dictatorship.

10. Intellectuals and students may become restless in response to conditions, restrictions, doctrinalism, and repression.

11. The general public may over time become apathetic, skeptical, and even hostile to the regime.

12. Regional, class, cultural, or national differences may become acute.

13. The power hierarchy of the dictatorship is always unstable to some degree, and at times extremely so. Individuals do not only remain in the same position in the ranking, but may rise or fall to other ranks or be removed entirely and replaced by new persons.

14. Sections of the police or military forces may act to achieve their own objectives, even against the will of established dictators, including by coup d'état.

15. If the dictatorship is new, time is required for it to become well established.

16. With so many decisions made by so few people in the dictatorship, mistakes of judgment, policy, and action are likely to occur.

17. If the regime seeks to avoid these dangers and decentralises controls and decision making, its control over the central levers of power may be further eroded.

Attacking weaknesses of dictatorships

With knowledge of such inherent weaknesses, the democratic opposition can seek to aggravate these

"Achilles' heels" deliberately in order to alter the system drastically or to disintegrate it.

The conclusion is then clear: despite the appearances of strength, all dictatorships have weaknesses, internal inefficiencies, personal rivalries, institutional inefficiencies, and conflicts between organisations and departments. These weaknesses, over time, tend to make the regime less effective and more vulnerable to changing conditions and deliberate resistance. Not everything the regime sets out to accomplish will get completed. At times, for example, even Hitler's direct orders were never implemented because those beneath him in the hierarchy refused to carry them out. The dictatorial regime may at times even fall apart quickly, as we have already observed.

This does not mean dictatorships can be destroyed without risks and casualties. Every possible course of action for liberation will involve risks and potential suffering, and will take time to operate. And, of course, no means of action can ensure rapid success in every situation. However, types of struggle that target the dictatorship's identifiable weaknesses have greater chance of success than those that seek to fight the dictatorship where it is clearly strongest. The question is how this struggle is to be waged.

Five

Exercising Power

In Chapter One we noted that military resistance against dictatorships does not strike them where they are weakest, but rather where they are strongest. By choosing to compete in the areas of military forces, supplies of ammunition, weapons technology, and the like, resistance movements tend to put themselves at a distinct disadvantage. Dictatorships will almost always be able to muster superior resources in these areas. The dangers of relying on foreign powers for salvation were also outlined. In Chapter Two we examined the problems of relying on negotiations as a means to remove dictatorships.

What means are then available that will offer the democratic resistance distinct advantages and will tend to aggravate the identified weaknesses of dictatorships? What technique of action will capitalise on the theory of political power discussed in Chapter Three? The alternative of choice is political defiance.

Political defiance has the following characteristics:

• It does not accept that the outcome will be decided by the means of fighting chosen by the dictatorship.

• It is difficult for the regime to combat.

• It can uniquely aggravate weaknesses of the dictatorship and can sever its sources of power.

• It can in action be widely dispersed but can also be concentrated on a specific objective.

• It leads to errors of judgment and action by the dictators.

• It can effectively utilise the population as a whole and the society's groups and institutions in the struggle to end the brutal domination of the few.

• It helps to spread the distribution of effective power in the society, making the establishment and maintenance of a democratic society more possible.

The workings of nonviolent struggle

Like military capabilities, political defiance can be employed for a variety of purposes, ranging from efforts to influence the opponents to take different actions, to create conditions for a peaceful resolution of conflict, or to disintegrate the opponents' regime. However, political defiance operates in quite different ways from violence. Although both techniques are means to wage struggle, they do so with very different means and with different consequences. The ways and results of violent conflict are well known. Physical weapons are used to intimidate, injure, kill, and destroy.

Nonviolent struggle is a much more complex and varied means of struggle than is violence. Instead, the struggle is fought by psychological, social, economic, and political weapons applied by the population and the institutions of the society. These have been known under various names of protests, strikes, noncooperation, boycotts, disaffection, and people power. As noted earlier, all governments can rule only as long as they receive replenishment of the needed sources of their power from the cooperation, submission, and obedience of the population and the institutions of the society. Political defiance, unlike violence, is uniquely suited to severing those sources of power.

Nonviolent weapons and discipline

The common error of past improvised political defiance campaigns is the reliance on only one or two methods, such as strikes and mass demonstrations. In fact, a multitude of methods exist that allow resistance strategists to concentrate and disperse resistance as required.

About two hundred specific methods of nonviolent action have been identified, and there are certainly scores more. These methods are classified under three broad categories: protest and persuasion, noncooperation, and intervention. Methods of nonviolent protest and persuasion are largely symbolic demonstrations, including parades, marches, and vigils (54 methods). Noncooperation is divided into three sub-categories: (A) social noncooperation (16 methods), (B) economic noncooperation, including boycotts (26 methods) and strikes (23 methods), and (C) political noncooperation (38 methods). Nonviolent intervention, by psychological, physical, social, economic, or political means, such as the fast, nonviolent occupation, and parallel government (41 methods), is the final group. A list of 198 of these methods is included as the Appendix to this publication.

The use of a considerable number of these methods – carefully chosen, applied persistently and on a large scale, wielded in the context of a wise strategy and appropriate tactics, by trained civilians – is likely to cause any illegitimate regime severe problems. This applies to all dictatorships.

In contrast to military means, the methods of nonviolent struggle can be focused directly on the issues at stake. For example, since the issue of dictatorship is primarily political, then political forms of nonviolent struggle would be crucial. These would include denial of legitimacy to the dictators and noncooperation with their regime. Noncooperation would also be applied against specific policies. At times stalling and procrastination may be quietly and even secretly practiced, while at other times open disobedience and defiant public demonstrations and strikes may be visible to all.

On the other hand, if the dictatorship is vulnerable to economic pressures or if many of the popular grievances against it are economic, then economic action, such as boycotts or strikes, may be appropriate resistance methods. The dictators' efforts to exploit the economic system might be met with limited general strikes, slow-downs, and refusal of assistance by (or disappearance of) indispensable experts. Selective use of various types of strikes may be conducted at key points in manufacturing, in transport, in the supply of raw materials, and in the distribution of products.

Some methods of nonviolent struggle require people to perform acts unrelated to their normal lives, such as distributing leaflets, operating an underground press, going on hunger strike, or sitting down in the streets. These methods may be difficult for some people to undertake except in very extreme situations.

Other methods of nonviolent struggle instead require people to continue approximately their normal lives, though in somewhat different ways. For example, people may report for work, instead of striking, but then deliberately work more slowly or inefficiently than usual. "Mistakes" may be consciously made more frequently. One may become "sick" and "unable" to work at certain times. Or, one may simply refuse to work. One might go to religious services when the act expresses not only religious but also political convictions. One may act to protect children from the attackers' propaganda by education at home or in illegal classes. One might refuse to join certain "recommended" or required organisations that one would not have joined freely in earlier times. The similarity of such types of action to people's usual activities and the limited degree of departure from their normal lives may make participation in the national liberation struggle much easier for many people.

Since nonviolent struggle and violence operate in fundamentally different ways, even limited resistance violence during a political defiance campaign will be counterproductive, for it will shift the struggle to one in which the dictators have an overwhelming advantage (military warfare). Nonviolent discipline is a key to success and must be maintained despite provocations and brutalities by the dictators and their agents.

The maintenance of nonviolent discipline against violent opponents facilitates the workings of the four mechanisms of change in nonviolent struggle (discussed below). Nonviolent discipline is also extremely important in the process of political jiu-jitsu. In this process the stark brutality of the regime against the clearly nonviolent actionists politically rebounds against the dictators' position, causing dissention in their own ranks as well as fomenting support for the resisters among the general population, the regime's usual supporters, and third parties.

In some cases, however, limited violence against the dictatorship may be inevitable. Frustration and hatred of the regime may explode into violence. Or, certain groups may be unwilling to abandon violent means even though they recognise the important role of nonviolent struggle. In these cases, political defiance does not need to be abandoned. However, it will be necessary to separate the violent action as far as possible from the nonviolent action. This should be done in terms of geography, population groups, timing, and issues. Otherwise the violence could have a disastrous effect on the potentially much more powerful and successful use of political defiance.

The historical record indicates that while casualties in dead and wounded must be expected in political defiance, they will be far fewer than the casualties in military warfare. Furthermore, this type of struggle does not contribute to the endless cycle of killing and brutality.

Nonviolent struggle both requires and tends to produce a loss (or greater control) of fear of the government and its violent repression. That abandonment or control of fear is a key element in destroying the power of the dictators over the general population.

Openness, secrecy, and high standards

Secrecy, deception, and underground conspiracy pose very difficult problems for a movement using nonviolent action. It is often impossible to keep the political police and intelligence agents from learning about intentions and plans. From the perspective of the movement, secrecy is not only rooted in fear but contributes to fear, which dampens the spirit of resistance and reduces the number of people who can participate in a given action. It also can contribute to suspicions and accusations, often unjustified, within the movement, concerning who is an informer or agent for the opponents. Secrecy may also affect the ability of a movement to remain nonviolent. In contrast, openness regarding intentions and plans will not only have the opposite effects, but will contribute to an image that the resistance movement is in fact extremely powerful. The problem is of course more complex than this suggests, and there are significant aspects of resistance activities that may require secrecy. A well-informed assessment will be required by those knowledgeable about both the dynamics of nonviolent struggle and also the dictatorship's means of surveillance in the specific situation.

The editing, printing, and distribution of underground publications, the use of illegal radio broadcasts from within the country, and the gathering of intelligence about the operations of the dictatorship are among the special limited types of activities where a high degree of secrecy will be required.

The maintenance of high standards of behavior in nonviolent action is necessary at all stages of the conflict. Such factors as fearlessness and maintaining nonviolent discipline are always required. It is important to remember that large numbers of people may frequently be necessary to effect particular changes. However, such numbers can be obtained as reliable participants only by maintaining the high standards of the movement.

Strategists need to remember that the conflict in which political defiance is applied is a constantly changing field of struggle with continuing interplay of moves and countermoves. Nothing is static. Power relationships, both absolute and relative, are subject to constant and rapid changes. This is made possible by the resisters continuing their nonviolent persistence despite repression.

The variations in the respective power of the contending sides in this type of conflict situation are likely to be more extreme than in violent conflicts, to take place more quickly, and to have more diverse and politically significant consequences. Due to these variations, specific actions by the resisters are likely to have consequences far beyond the particular time and place in which they occur. These effects will rebound to strengthen or weaken one group or another.

In addition, the nonviolent group may, by its actions exert influence over the increase or decrease in the relative strength of the opponent group to a great extent. For example, disciplined courageous nonviolent resistance in face of the dictators' brutalities may induce unease, disaffection, unreliability, and in extreme situations even mutiny among the dictators' own soldiers and population. This resistance may also result in increased international condemnation of the dictatorship. In addition, skillful, disciplined, and persistent use of political defiance may result in more and more participation in the resistance by people who normally would give their tacit support to the dictators or generally remain neutral in the conflict.

Four mechanisms of change

Nonviolent struggle produces change in four ways. The first mechanism is the least likely, though it has occurred. When members of the opponent group are emotionally moved by the suffering of repression imposed on courageous nonviolent resisters or are rationally persuaded that the resisters' cause is just, they may come to accept the resisters' aims. This mechanism is called conversion. Though cases of conversion in nonviolent action do sometimes happen, they are rare, and in most conflicts this does not occur at all or at least not on a significant scale.

Far more often, nonviolent struggle operates by changing the conflict situation and the society so that the opponents simply cannot do as they like. It is this change that produces the other three mechanisms: accommodation, nonviolent coercion, and disintegration. Which of these occurs depends on the degree to which the relative and absolute power relations are shifted in favour of the democrats.

If the issues are not fundamental ones, the demands of the opposition in a limited campaign are not considered threatening, and the contest of forces has altered the power relationships to some degree, the immediate conflict may be ended by reaching an agreement, a splitting of differences or compromise. This mechanism is called accommodation. Many strikes are settled in this manner, for example, with both sides attaining some of their objectives but neither achieving all it wanted. A government may perceive such a settlement to have some positive benefits, such as defusing tension, creating an impression of "fairness," or polishing the international image of the regime. It is important, therefore, that great care be exercised in selecting the issues on which a settlement by accommodation is acceptable. A struggle to bring down a dictatorship is not one of these.

Nonviolent struggle can be much more powerful than indicated by the mechanisms of conversion or accommodation. Mass noncooperation and defiance can so change social and political situations, especially power relationships, that the dictators' ability to control the economic, social, and political processes of government and the society is in fact taken away. The opponents' military forces may become so unreliable that they no longer simply obey orders to repress resisters. Although the opponents' leaders remain in their positions, and adhere to their original goals, their ability to act effectively has been taken away from them. That is called nonviolent coercion.

In some extreme situations, the conditions producing nonviolent coercion are carried still further. The opponents' leadership in fact loses all ability to act and their own structure of power collapses. The resisters' self-direction, noncooperation, and defiance become so complete that the opponents now lack even a semblance of control over them. The opponents' bureaucracy refuses to obey its own leadership. The opponents' troops and police mutiny. The opponents' usual supporters or population repudiate their former leadership, denying that they have any right to rule at all. Hence, their former assistance and obedience falls away. The fourth mechanism of change, *disintegration* of the opponents' system, is so complete that they do not even have sufficient power to surrender. The regime simply falls to pieces.

In planning liberation strategies, these four mechanisms should be kept in mind. They sometimes operate essentially by chance. However, the selection of one or more of these as the intended mechanism of change in a conflict will make it possible to formulate specific and mutually reinforcing strategies. Which mechanism (or mechanisms) to select will depend on numerous factors, including the absolute and relative power of the contending groups and the attitudes and objectives of the nonviolent struggle group.

Democratising effects of political defiance

In contrast to the centralising effects of violent sanctions, use of the technique of nonviolent struggle contributes to democratising the political society in several ways.

One part of the democratising effect is negative. That is, in contrast to military means, this technique does not provide a means of repression under command of a ruling elite which can be turned against the population to establish or maintain a dictatorship. Leaders of a political defiance movement can exert influence and apply pressures on their followers, but they cannot imprison or execute them when they dissent or choose other leaders.

Another part of the democratising effect is positive. That is, nonviolent struggle provides the population with means of resistance that can be used to achieve and defend their liberties against existing or would-be dictators. Below are several of the positive democratising effects nonviolent struggle may have:

• Experience in applying nonviolent struggle may result in the population being more self-confident in challenging the regime's threats and capacity for violent repression.

• Nonviolent struggle provides the means of non-cooperation and defiance by which the population can resist undemocratic controls over them by any dictatorial group.

• Nonviolent struggle can be used to assert the practice

of democratic freedoms, such as free speech, free press, independent organisations, and free assembly, in face of repressive controls.

• Nonviolent struggle contributes strongly to the survival, rebirth, and strengthening of the independent groups and institutions of the society, as previously discussed. These are important for democracy because of their capacity to mobilise the power capacity of the population and to impose limits on the effective power of any would-be dictators.

• Nonviolent struggle provides means by which the population can wield power against repressive police and military action by a dictatorial government.

• Nonviolent struggle provides methods by which the population and the independent institutions can in the interests of democracy restrict or sever the sources of power for the ruling elite, thereby threatening its capacity to continue its domination.

Complexity of nonviolent struggle

As we have seen from this discussion, nonviolent struggle is a complex technique of social action, involving a multitude of methods, a range of mechanisms of change, and specific behavioral requirements. To be effective, especially against a dictatorship, political defiance requires careful planning and preparation. Prospective participants will need to understand what is required of them. Resources will need to have been made available. And strategists will need to have analyzed how non-violent struggle can be most effectively applied. We now turn our attention to this latter crucial element: the need for strategic planning.

Six

The Need for Strategic Planning

Political defiance campaigns against dictatorships may begin in a variety of ways. In the past these struggles have almost always been unplanned and essentially accidental. Specific grievances that have triggered past initial actions have varied widely, but often included new brutalities, the arrest or killing of a highly regarded person, a new repressive policy or order, food shortages, disrespect toward religious beliefs, or an anniversary of an important related event. Sometimes, a particular act by the dictatorship has so enraged the populace that they have launched into action without having any idea how the rising might end. At other times a courageous individual or a small group may have taken action which aroused support. A specific grievance may be recognised by others as similar to wrongs they had experienced and they, too, may thus join the struggle. Sometimes, a specific call for resistance from a small group or individual may meet an unexpectedly large response.

While spontaneity has some positive qualities, it has often had disadvantages. Frequently, the democratic resisters have not anticipated the brutalities of the dictatorship, so that they suffered gravely and the resistance has collapsed. At times the lack of planning by democrats has left crucial decisions to chance, with disastrous results. Even when the oppressive system was brought down, lack of planning on how to handle the transition to a democratic system has contributed to the emergence of a new dictatorship.

Realistic planning

In the future, unplanned popular action will undoubtedly play significant roles in risings against dictatorships. However, it is now possible to calculate the most effective ways to bring down a dictatorship, to assess when the political situation and popular mood are ripe, and to choose how to initiate a campaign. Very careful thought *based on a realistic assessment* of the situation and the capabilities of the populace is required in order to select effective ways to achieve freedom under such circumstances.

If one wishes to accomplish something, it is wise to plan how to do it. The more important the goal, or the graver the consequences of failure, the more important planning becomes. Strategic planning increases the likelihood that all available resources will be mobilised and employed most effectively. This is especially true for a democratic movement – which has limited material resources and whose supporters will be in danger – that is trying to bring down a powerful dictatorship. In contrast, the dictatorship usually will have access to vast material resources, organisational strength, and ability to perpetrate brutalities.

"To plan a strategy" here means to calculate a course of action that will make it more likely to get from the present to the desired future situation. In terms of this discussion, it means from a dictatorship to a future democratic system. A plan to achieve that objective will usually consist of a phased series of campaigns and other organised activities designed to strengthen the oppressed population and society and to weaken the dictatorship. Note here that the objective is not simply to destroy the current dictatorship but to emplace a democratic system. A grand strategy that limits its objective to merely destroying the incumbent dictatorship runs a great risk of producing another tyrant.

Hurdles to planning

Some exponents of freedom in various parts of the world do not bring their full capacities to bear on the problem of how to achieve liberation. Only rarely do these advocates fully recognise the extreme importance of careful strategic planning before they act. Consequently, this is almost never done.

Why is it that the people who have the vision of bringing political freedom to their people should so rarely prepare a comprehensive strategic plan to achieve that goal? Unfortunately, often most people in democratic opposition groups do not understand the need for strategic planning or are not accustomed or trained to think strategically. This is a difficult task. Constantly harassed by the dictatorship, and over-whelmed by immediate responsibilities, resistance leaders often do not have the safety or time to develop strategic thinking skills.

Instead, it is a common pattern simply to react to the initiatives of the dictatorship. The opposition is then always on the defensive, seeking to maintain limited liberties or bastions of freedom, at best slowing the advance of the dictatorial controls or causing certain problems for the regime's new policies.

Some individuals and groups, of course, may not see the need for broad long-term planning of a liberation movement. Instead, they may naïvely think that if they simply espouse their goal strongly, firmly, and long enough, it will somehow come to pass. Others assume that if they simply live and witness according to their principles and ideals in face of difficulties, they are doing all they can to implement them. The espousal of humane goals and loyalty to ideals are admirable, but are grossly inadequate to end a dictatorship and to achieve freedom.

Other opponents of dictatorship may naïvely think that if only they use enough violence, freedom will come. But, as noted earlier, violence is no guarantor of success. Instead of liberation, it can lead to defeat, massive tragedy, or both. In most situations the dictatorship is best equipped for violent struggle and the military realities rarely, if ever, favour the democrats.

There are also activists who base their actions on

what they "feel" they should do. These approaches are, however, not only egocentric but they offer no guidance for developing a grand strategy of liberation.

Action based on a "bright idea" that someone has had is also limited. What is needed instead is action based on careful calculation of the "next steps" required to topple the dictatorship. Without strategic analysis, resistance leaders will often not know what that "next step" should be, for they have not thought carefully about the successive specific steps required to achieve victory. Creativity and bright ideas are very important, but they need to be utilised in order to advance the strategic situation of the democratic forces.

Acutely aware of the multitude of actions that could be taken against the dictatorship and unable to determine where to begin, some people counsel "Do everything simultaneously." That might be helpful but, of course, is impossible, especially for relatively weak movements. Furthermore, such an approach provides no guidance on where to begin, on where to concentrate efforts, and how to use often limited resources.

Other persons and groups may see the need for some planning, but are only able to think about it on a short-term or tactical basis. They may not see that longer-term planning is necessary or possible. They may at times be unable to think and analyze in strategic terms, allowing themselves to be repeatedly distracted by relatively small issues, often responding to the opponents' actions rather than seizing the initiative for the democratic resistance. Devoting so much energy to short-term activities, these leaders often fail to explore several alternative courses of action which could guide the overall efforts so that the goal is constantly approached.

It is also just possible that some democratic movements do not plan a comprehensive strategy to bring down the dictatorship, concentrating instead only on immediate issues, for another reason. Inside themselves, they do not really believe that the dictatorship can be ended by their own efforts. Therefore, planning how to do so is considered to be a romantic waste of time or an exercise in futility. People struggling for freedom against established brutal dictatorships are often confronted by such immense military and police power that it appears the dictators can accomplish whatever they will. Lacking real hope, these people will, nevertheless, defy the dictatorship for reasons of integrity and perhaps history. Though they will never admit it, perhaps never consciously recognise it, their actions appear to themselves as hopeless. Hence, for them, long-term comprehensive strategic planning has no merit.

The result of such failures to plan strategically is often drastic: one's strength is dissipated, one's actions are ineffective, energy is wasted on minor issues, advantages are not utilised, and sacrifices are for naught. If democrats do not plan strategically they are likely to fail to achieve their objectives. A poorly planned, odd mixture of activities will not move a major resistance effort forward. Instead, it will more likely allow the dictatorship to increase its controls and power.

Unfortunately, because comprehensive strategic plans for liberation are rarely, if ever, developed, dictatorships appear much more durable than they in fact are. They survive for years or decades longer than need be the case.

Four important terms in strategic planning

In order to help us to think strategically, clarity about the meanings of four basic terms is important.

Grand strategy is the conception that serves to coordinate and direct the use of all appropriate and available resources (economic, human, moral, political, organisational, etc.) of a group seeking to attain its objectives in a conflict.

Grand strategy, by focusing primary attention on the group's objectives and resources in the conflict, determines the most appropriate technique of action (such as conventional military warfare or nonviolent struggle) to be employed in the conflict. In planning a grand strategy resistance leaders must evaluate and plan which pressures and influences are to be brought to bear upon the opponents. Further, grand strategy will include decisions on the appropriate conditions and timing under which initial and subsequent resistance campaigns will be launched.

Grand strategy sets the basic framework for the selection of more limited strategies for waging the struggle. Grand strategy also determines the allocation of general tasks to particular groups and the distribution of resources to them for use in the struggle.

Strategy is the conception of how best to achieve particular objectives in a conflict, operating within the scope of the chosen grand strategy. Strategy is concerned with whether, when, and how to fight, as well as how to achieve maximum effectiveness in struggling for certain ends. A strategy has been compared to the artist's concept, while a strategic plan is the architect's blueprint.[12]

Strategy may also include efforts to develop a strategic situation that is so advantageous that the opponents are able to foresee that open conflict is likely to bring their certain defeat, and therefore capitulate without an open struggle. Or, if not, the improved strategic situation will make success of the challengers certain in struggle. Strategy also involves how to act to make good use of successes when gained.

Applied to the course of the struggle itself, the strategic plan is the basic idea of how a campaign shall develop, and how its separate components shall be fitted together to contribute most advantageously to achieve its objectives. It involves the skillful deployment of particular action groups in smaller operations. Planning for a wise strategy must take into consideration the requirements for success in the operation of the chosen technique of struggle. Different techniques will have different requirements. Of course, just fulfilling "requirements" is not sufficient to ensure success. Additional factors may also be needed.

In devising strategies, the democrats must clearly define their objectives and determine how to measure the effectiveness of efforts to achieve them. This definition and analysis permits the strategist to identify the precise requirements for securing each selected objective. This need for clarity and definition applies equally to tactical planning.

Tactics and methods of action are used to implement the strategy. *Tactics* relate to the skillful use of one's forces to the best advantage in a limited situation. A tactic is a limited action, employed to achieve a restricted objective. The choice of tactics is governed by the conception of how best in a restricted phase of a conflict to utilise the available means of fighting to implement the strategy. To be most effective, tactics and methods must be chosen and applied with constant attention to the achievement of strategic objectives. Tactical gains that do not reinforce the attainment of strategic objectives may in the end turn out to be wasted energy.

A tactic is thus concerned with a limited course of action that fits within the broad strategy, just as a strategy fits within the grand strategy. Tactics are always concerned with fighting, whereas strategy includes wider considerations. A particular tactic can only be understood as part of the overall strategy of a battle or a campaign. Tactics are applied for shorter periods of time than strategies, or in smaller areas (geographical, institutional, etc.), or by a more limited number of people, or for more limited objectives. In nonviolent action the distinction between a tactical objective and a strategic objective may be partly indicated by whether the chosen objective of the action is minor or major.

Offensive tactical engagements are selected to support attainment of strategic objectives. Tactical engagements are the tools of the strategist in creating conditions favourable for delivering decisive attacks against an opponent. It is most important, therefore, that those given responsibility for planning and executing tactical operations be skilled in assessing the situation, and selecting the most appropriate methods for it. Those expected to participate must be trained in the use of the chosen technique and the specific methods.

Method refers to the specific weapons or means of action. Within the technique of nonviolent struggle, these include the dozens of particular forms of action (such as the many kinds of strikes, boycotts, political noncooperation, and the like) cited in Chapter Five (see also Appendix.)

The development of a responsible and effective strategic plan for a nonviolent struggle depends upon the careful formulation and selection of the grand strategy, strategies, tactics, and methods.

The main lesson of this discussion is that a calculated use of one's intellect is required in careful strategic planning for liberation from a dictatorship. Failure to plan intelligently can contribute to disasters, while the effective use of one's intellectual capacities can chart a strategic course that will judiciously utilise one's available resources to move the society toward the goal of liberty and democracy.

Seven

Planning Strategy

In order to increase the chances for success, resistance leaders will need to formulate a comprehensive plan of action capable of strengthening the suffering people, weakening and then destroying the dictatorship, and building a durable democracy. To achieve such a plan of action, a careful assessment of the situation and of the options for effective action is needed. Out of such a careful analysis both a grand strategy and the specific campaign strategies for achieving freedom can be developed. Though related, the development of grand strategy and campaign strategies are two separate processes. Only after the grand strategy has been developed can the specific campaign strategies be fully developed. Campaign strategies will need to be designed to achieve and reinforce the grand strategic objectives.

The development of resistance strategy requires attention to many questions and tasks. Here we shall identify some of the important factors that need to be considered, both at the grand strategic level and the level of campaign strategy. All strategic planning, however, requires that the resistance planners have a profound understanding of the entire conflict situation, including attention to physical, historical, governmental, military, cultural, social, political, psychological, economic, and international factors. Strategies can only be developed in the context of the particular struggle and its background.

Of primary importance, democratic leaders and strategic planners will want to assess the objectives and importance of the cause. Are the objectives worth a major struggle, and why? It is critical to determine the real objective of the struggle. We have argued here that overthrow of the dictatorship or removal of the present dictators is *not* enough. The objective in these conflicts needs to be the establishment of a free society with a democratic system of government. Clarity on this point will influence the development of a grand strategy and of the ensuing specific strategies.

Particularly, strategists will need to answer many fundamental questions, such as these:

• What are the main obstacles to achieving freedom?

• What factors will facilitate achieving freedom?

• What are the main strengths of the dictatorship?

• What are the various weaknesses of the dictatorship?

• To what degree are the sources of power for the dictatorship vulnerable?

• What are the strengths of the democratic forces and the general population?

• What are the weaknesses of the democratic forces and how can they be corrected?

• What is the status of third parties, not immediately involved in the conflict, who already assist or might assist, either the dictatorship or the democratic movement, and if so in what ways?

Choice of means

At the grand strategic level, planners will need to choose the main means of struggle to be employed in the coming conflict. The merits and limitations of several alternative techniques of struggle will need to be evaluated, such as conventional military warfare, guerrilla warfare, political defiance, and others.

In making this choice the strategists will need to consider such questions as the following: Is the chosen type of struggle within the capacities of the democrats? Does the chosen technique utilise strengths of the dominated population? Does this technique target the weaknesses of the dictatorship, or does it strike at its strongest points? Do the means help the democrats become more self-reliant, or do they require dependency on third parties or external suppliers? What is the record of the use of the chosen means in bringing down dictatorships? Do they increase or limit the casualties and destruction that may be incurred in the coming conflict? Assuming success in ending the dictatorship, what effect would the selected means have on the type of government that would arise from the struggle? The types of action determined to be counterproductive will need to be excluded in the developed grand strategy.

In previous chapters we have argued that political defiance offers significant comparative advantages to other techniques of struggle. Strategists will need to examine their particular conflict situation and determine whether political defiance provides affirmative answers to the above questions.

Planning for democracy

It should be remembered that against a dictatorship the objective of the grand strategy is not simply to bring down the dictators but to install a democratic system and make the rise of a new dictatorship impossible. To accomplish these objectives, the chosen means of struggle will need to contribute to a change in the distribution of effective power in the society. Under the dictatorship the population and civil institutions of the society have been too weak, and the government too strong. Without a change in this imbalance, a new set of rulers can, if they wish, be just as dictatorial as the old ones. A "palace revolution" or a coup d'état therefore is not welcome.

Political defiance contributes to a more equitable distribution of effective power through the mobilisation of the society against the dictatorship, as was discussed in Chapter Five. This process occurs in several ways. The development of a nonviolent struggle capacity means that the dictatorship's capacity for violent repression no longer as easily produces intimidation and submission among the population. The population will have at its disposal powerful means to counter and at times block the exertion of the dictators' power. Further, the mobilisation of popular power through political defiance will strengthen the independent institutions of the society. The experience of once exercising effective power is not quickly forgot. The knowledge and skill gained in struggle will make the population less likely to be easily dominated by would-be dictators. This shift in power relationships would ultimately make establishment of a durable democratic society much more likely.

External assistance

As part of the preparation of a grand strategy it is necessary to assess what will be the relative roles of internal resistance and external pressures for dis-integrating the dictatorship. In this analysis we have argued that the main force of the struggle must be borne from inside the country itself. To the degree that international assistance comes at all, it will be stimulated by the internal struggle.

As a modest supplement, efforts can be made to mobilise world public opinion against the dictatorship, on humanitarian, moral, and religious grounds. Efforts can be taken to obtain diplomatic, political, and economic sanctions by governments and international organisations against the dictatorship. These may take the forms of economic and military weapons embargoes, reduction in levels of diplomatic recognition or the breaking of diplomatic ties, banning of economic assistance and prohibition of investments in the dictatorial country, expulsion of the dictatorial government from various international organisations and from United Nations bodies. Further, international assistance, such as the provision of financial and communications support, can also be provided directly to the democratic forces.

Formulating a grand strategy

Following an assessment of the situation, the choice of means, and a determination of the role of external assistance, planners of the grand strategy will need to sketch in broad strokes how the conflict might best be conducted. This broad plan would stretch from the present to the future liberation and the institution of a democratic system.

In formulating a grand strategy these planners will need to ask themselves a variety of questions. The following questions pose (in a more specific way than earlier) the types of considerations required in devising a grand strategy for a political defiance struggle:

How might the long-term struggle best begin? How can the oppressed population muster sufficient self-confidence and strength to act to challenge the dictatorship, even initially in a limited way? How could the population's capacity to apply noncooperation and defiance be increased with time and experience? What might be the objectives of a series of limited campaigns to regain democratic control over the society and limit the dictatorship?

Are there independent institutions that have survived the dictatorship which might be used in the struggle to establish freedom? What institutions of the society can be regained from the dictators' control, or what institutions need to be newly created by the democrats to meet their needs and establish spheres of democracy even while the dictatorship continues?

How can organisational strength in the resistance be developed? How can participants be trained? What resources (finances, equipment, etc.) will be required throughout the struggle? What types of symbolism can be most effective in mobilising the population?

By what kinds of action and in what stages could the sources of power of the dictators be incrementally weakened and severed? How can the resisting population simultaneously persist in its defiance and also maintain the necessary nonviolent discipline? How can the society continue to meet its basic needs during the course of the struggle? How can social order be maintained in the midst of the conflict? As victory approaches, how can the democratic resistance continue to build the institutional base of the post-dictatorship society to make the transition as smooth as possible?

It must be remembered that no single blueprint exists or can be created to plan strategy for every liberation movement against dictatorships. Each struggle to bring down a dictatorship and establish a democratic system will be somewhat different. No two situations will be exactly alike, each dictatorship will have some individual characteristics, and the capacities of the freedom-seeking population will vary. Planners of grand strategy for a political defiance struggle will require a profound understanding not only of their specific conflict situation, but of their chosen means of struggle as well.[13]

When the grand strategy of the struggle has been carefully planned there are sound reasons for making it widely known. The large numbers of people required to participate may be more willing and able to act if they understand the general conception, as well as specific instructions. This knowledge could potentially have a very positive effect on their morale, their willingness to participate, and to act appropriately. The general outlines of the grand strategy would become known to the dictators in any case and knowledge of its features potentially could lead them to be less brutal in their repression, knowing that it could rebound politically against themselves. Awareness of the special characteristics of the grand strategy could potentially also contribute to dissension and defections from the dictators' own camp.

Once a grand strategic plan for bringing down the dictatorship and establishing a democratic system has been adopted, it is important for the pro-democracy groups to persist in applying it. Only in very rare circumstances should the struggle depart from the initial grand strategy. When there is abundant evidence that the chosen grand strategy was misconceived, or that the circumstances of the struggle have fundamentally changed, planners may need to alter the grand strategy. Even then, this should be done only after a basic reassessment has been made and a new more adequate grand strategic plan has been developed and adopted.

Planning campaign strategies

However wise and promising the developed grand strategy to end the dictatorship and to institute democracy may be, a grand strategy does not implement itself. Particular strategies will need to be developed to guide the major campaigns aimed at undermining the dictators' power. These strategies, in turn, will incorporate and guide a range of tactical engagements that will aim to strike decisive blows against the dictators' regime. The tactics and the specific methods of action must be chosen carefully so that they contribute to achieving the goals of each particular strategy. The discussion here focuses exclusively on the level of strategy.

Strategists planning the major campaigns will, like those who planned the grand strategy, require a thorough understanding of the nature and modes of operation of their chosen technique of struggle. Just as military officers must understand force structures, tactics, logistics, munitions, the effects of geography, and the like in order to plot military strategy, political defiance planners must understand the nature and strategic principles of nonviolent struggle. Even then, however, knowledge of nonviolent struggle, attention to recommendations in this essay, and answers to the questions posed here will not themselves produce strategies. The formulation of strategies for the struggle still requires an informed creativity.

In planning the strategies for the specific selective resistance campaigns and for the longer term development of the liberation struggle, the political defiance strategists will need to consider various issues and problems. The following are among these:

• Determination of the specific objectives of the campaign and their contributions to implementing the grand strategy.

• Consideration of the specific methods, or political weapons, that can best be used to implement the chosen strategies. Within each overall plan for a particular strategic campaign it will be necessary to determine what smaller, tactical plans and which specific methods of action should be used to impose pressures and restrictions against the dictatorship's sources of power. It should be remembered that the achievement of major objectives will come as a result of carefully chosen and implemented specific smaller steps.

• Determination whether, or how, economic issues should be related to the overall essentially political struggle. If economic issues are to be prominent in the struggle, care will be needed that the economic grievances can actually be remedied after the dictatorship is ended. Otherwise, disillusionment and disaffection may set in if quick solutions are not provided during the transition period to a democratic society. Such disillusionment could facilitate the rise of dictatorial forces promising an end to economic woes.

• Determination in advance of what kind of leadership structure and communications system will work best for initiating the resistance struggle. What means of decision-making and communication will be possible during the course of the struggle to give continuing guidance to the resisters and the general population?

• Communication of the resistance news to the general population, to the dictators' forces, and the international press. Claims and reporting should always be strictly factual. Exaggerations and unfounded claims will undermine the credibility of the resistance.

• Plans for self-reliant constructive social, educational, economic, and political activities to meet the needs of one's own people during the coming conflict. Such projects can be conducted by persons not directly involved in the resistance activities.

• Determination of what kind of external assistance is desirable in support of the specific campaign or the general liberation struggle. How can external help be best mobilised and used without making the internal struggle dependent on uncertain external factors? Attention will need to be given to which external groups are most likely, and most appropriate, to assist, such as non-governmental organisations (social movements, religious or political groups, labour unions, etc.), governments, and/or the United Nations and its various bodies.

Furthermore, the resistance planners will need to take measures to preserve order and to meet social needs by one's own forces during mass resistance against dictatorial controls. This will not only create alternative independent democratic structures and meet genuine needs, but also will reduce credibility for any claims that ruthless repression is required to halt disorder and lawlessness.

For successful political defiance against a dictatorship, it is essential that the population grasp the idea of noncooperation. As illustrated by the "Monkey Master" story (see Chapter Three), the basic idea is simple: if enough of the subordinates refuse to continue their cooperation long enough despite repression, the oppressive system will be weakened and finally collapse.

People living under the dictatorship may be already familiar with this concept from a variety of sources. Even so, the democratic forces should deliberately spread and popularise the idea of noncooperation. The "Monkey Master" story, or a similar one, could be disseminated throughout the society. Such a story could be easily understood. Once the general concept of noncooperation is grasped, people will be able to understand the relevance of future calls to practice noncooperation with the dictatorship. They will also be able on their own to improvise a myriad of specific forms of noncooperation in new situations.

Despite the difficulties and dangers in attempts to communicate ideas, news, and resistance instructions while living under dictatorships, democrats have frequently proved this to be possible. Even under Nazi and Communist rule it was possible for resisters to communicate not only with other individuals but even with large public audiences through the production of illegal newspapers, leaflets, books, and in later years with audio and video cassettes.

With the advantage of prior strategic planning, general guidelines for resistance can be prepared and disseminated. These can indicate the issues and circumstances under which the population should protest and withhold cooperation, and how this might be done. Then, even if communications from the democratic leadership are severed, and specific instructions have not been issued or received, the population will know how to act on certain important issues. Such guidelines would also provide a test to identify counterfeit "resistance instructions" issued by the political police designed to provoke discrediting action.

Repression and countermeasures

Strategic planners will need to assess the likely responses and repression, especially the threshold of violence, of the dictatorship to the actions of the democratic resistance. It will be necessary to determine how to withstand, counteract, or avoid this possible increased repression without submission. Tactically, for specific occasions, appropriate warnings to the population and the resisters about expected repression would be in order, so that they will know the risks of participation. If repression may be serious, preparations for medical assistance for wounded resisters should be made.

Anticipating repression, the strategists will do well to consider in advance the use of tactics and methods that will contribute to achieving the specific goal of a campaign, or liberation, but that will make brutal repression less likely or less possible. For example, street demonstrations and parades against extreme dictatorships may be dramatic, but they may also risk thousands of dead demonstrators. The high cost to the demonstrators may not, however, actually apply more pressure on the dictatorship than would occur through everyone staying home, a strike, or massive acts of noncooperation from the civil servants.

If it has been proposed that provocative resistance action risking high casualties will be required for a strategic purpose, then one should very carefully consider the proposal's costs and possible gains. Will the population and the resisters be likely to behave in a disciplined and nonviolent manner during the course of the struggle? Can they resist provocations to violence? Planners must consider what measures may be taken to keep nonviolent discipline and maintain the resistance despite brutalities. Will such measures as pledges, policy statements, discipline leaflets, marshals for demonstrations, and boycotts of pro-violence persons and groups be possible and effective? Leaders should always be alert for the presence of *agents provocateurs* whose mission will be to incite the demonstrators to violence.

Adhering to the strategic plan

Once a sound strategic plan is in place, the democratic forces should not be distracted by minor moves of the dictators that may tempt them to depart from the grand strategy and the strategy for a particular campaign, causing them to focus major activities on unimportant issues. Nor should the emotions of the moment – perhaps in response to new brutalities by the dictatorship – be allowed to divert the democratic resistance from its grand strategy or the campaign strategy. The brutalities may have been perpetrated precisely in order to provoke the democratic forces to abandon their well-laid plan and even to commit violent acts in order that the dictators could more easily defeat them.

As long as the basic analysis is judged to be sound, the task of the pro-democracy forces is to press forward stage by stage. Of course, changes in tactics and intermediate objectives will occur and good leaders will always be ready to exploit opportunities. These adjustments should not be confused with objectives of the grand strategy or the objectives of the specific campaign. Careful implementation of the chosen grand strategy and of strategies for particular campaigns will greatly contribute to success.

Eight

Applying Political Defiance

In situations in which the population feels powerless and frightened, it is important that initial tasks for the public be low-risk, confidence-building actions. These types of actions – such as wearing one's clothes in an unusual way – may publicly register a dissenting opinion and provide an opportunity for the public to participate significantly in acts of dissent. In other cases a relatively minor (on the surface) nonpolitical issue (such as securing a safe water supply) might be made the focus for group action. Strategists should choose an issue the merits of which will be widely recognised and difficult to reject. Success in such limited campaigns could not only correct specific grievances but also convince the population that it indeed has power potential.

Most of the strategies of campaigns in the long-term struggle should *not* aim for the immediate complete downfall of the dictatorship, but instead for gaining limited objectives. Nor does every campaign require the participation of all sections of the population.

In contemplating a series of specific campaigns to implement the grand strategy, the defiance strategists need to consider how the campaigns at the beginning, the middle, and near the conclusion of the long-term struggle will differ from each other.

In the initial stages of the struggle, separate campaigns with different specific objectives can be very useful. Such selective campaigns may follow one after the other. Occasionally, two or three might overlap in time.

In planning a strategy for "selective resistance" it is necessary to identify specific limited issues or grievances that symbolise the general oppression of the dictatorship. Such issues may be the appropriate targets for conducting campaigns to gain intermediary strategic objectives within the overall grand strategy.

These intermediary strategic objectives need to be attainable by the current or projected power capacity of the democratic forces. This helps to ensure a series of victories, which are good for morale, and also contribute to advantageous incremental shifts in power relations for the long-term struggle.

Selective resistance strategies should concentrate primarily on specific social, economic, or political issues. These may be chosen in order to keep some part of the social and political system out of the dictators' control, to regain control of some part currently controlled by the dictators, or to deny the dictators a particular objective. If possible, the campaign of selective resistance should also strike at one weakness or more of the dictatorship, as already discussed. Thereby, democrats can make the greatest possible impact with their available power capacity.

Very early the strategists need to plan at least the strategy for the first campaign. What are to be its limited objectives? How will it help fulfill the chosen grand strategy? If possible, it is wise to formulate at least the general outlines of strategies for a second and possibly a third campaign. All such strategies will need to implement the chosen grand strategy and operate within its general guidelines.

Symbolic challenge

At the beginning of a new campaign to undermine the dictatorship, the first more specifically political actions may be limited in scope. They should be designed in part to test and influence the mood of the population, and to prepare them for continuing struggle through noncooperation and political defiance.

The initial action is likely to take the form of symbolic protest or may be a symbolic act of limited or temporary noncooperation. If the number of persons willing to act is small, then the initial act might, for example, involve placing flowers at a place of symbolic importance. On the other hand, if the number of persons willing to act is very large, then a five minute halt to all activities or several minutes of silence might be used. In other situations, a few individuals might undertake a hunger strike, a vigil at a place of symbolic importance, a brief student boycott of classes, or a temporary sit-in at an important office. Under a dictatorship these more aggressive actions would most likely be met with harsh repression.

Certain symbolic acts, such as a physical occupation in front of the dictator's palace or political police headquarters may involve high risk and are therefore not advisable for initiating a campaign.

Initial symbolic protest actions have at times aroused major national and international attention – as the mass street demonstrations in Burma in 1988 or the student occupation and hunger strike in Tiananman Square in Beijing in 1989. The high casualties of demonstrators in both of these cases points to the great care strategists must exercise in planning campaigns. Although having a tremendous moral and psychological impact, such actions by themselves are unlikely to bring down a dictatorship, for they remain largely symbolic and do not alter the power position of the dictatorship.

It usually is not possible to sever the availability of the sources of power to the dictators completely and rapidly at the beginning of a struggle. That would require virtually the whole population and almost all the institutions of the society – which had previously been largely submissive – to reject absolutely the regime and suddenly defy it by massive and strong noncooperation. That has not yet occurred and would be most difficult to achieve. In most cases, therefore, a quick campaign of full noncooperation and defiance is an unrealistic strategy for an early campaign against the dictatorship.

During a selective resistance campaign the brunt of the struggle is for a time usually borne by one section or more of the population. In a later campaign with a different objective, the burden of the struggle would be shifted to other population groups. For example, students might conduct strikes on an educational issue, religious leaders and believers might concentrate on a freedom of religion issue, rail workers might meticulously obey safety regulations so as to slow down the rail transport system, journalists might challenge censorship by publishing papers with blank spaces in which prohibited articles would have appeared, or police might repeatedly fail to locate and arrest wanted members of the democratic opposition. Phasing resistance campaigns by issue and population group will allow certain segments of the population to rest while resistance continues.

Selective resistance is especially important *to defend* the existence and autonomy of independent social, economic, and political groups and institutions outside the control of the dictatorship, which were briefly discussed earlier. These centres of power provide the institutional bases from which the population can exert pressure or can resist dictatorial controls. In the struggle, they are likely to be among the first targets of the dictatorship.

As the long-term struggle develops beyond the initial strategies into more ambitious and advanced phases, the strategists will need to calculate how the dictators' sources of power can be further restricted. The aim would be to use popular noncooperation to create a new more advantageous strategic situation for the democratic forces.

As the democratic resistance forces gained strength, strategists would plot more ambitious noncooperation and defiance to sever the dictatorships' sources of power, with the goal of producing increasing political paralysis, and in the end the disintegration of the dictatorship itself.

It will be necessary to plan carefully how the democratic forces can weaken the support that people and groups have previously offered to the dictatorship. Will their support be weakened by revelations of the brutalities perpetrated by the regime, by exposure of the disastrous economic consequences of the dictators' policies, or by a new understanding that the dictatorship can be ended? The dictators' supporters should at least be induced to become "neutral" in their activities ("fence sitters") or preferably to become active supporters of the movement for democracy.

During the planning and implementation of political defiance and noncooperation, it is highly important to pay close attention to all of the dictators' main supporters and aides, including their inner clique, political party, police, and bureaucrats, but especially their army.

The degree of loyalty of the military forces, both soldiers and officers, to the dictatorship needs to be carefully assessed and a determination should be made as to whether the military is open to influence by the democratic forces. Might many of the ordinary soldiers be unhappy and frightened conscripts? Might many of the soldiers and officers be alienated from the regime for personal, family, or political reasons? What other factors might make soldiers and officers vulnerable to democratic subversion?

Early in the liberation struggle a special strategy should be developed to communicate with the dictators' troops and functionaries. By words, symbols, and actions, the democratic forces can inform the troops that the liberation struggle will be vigourous, determined, and persistent. Troops should learn that the struggle will be of a special character, designed to undermine the dictatorship but not to threaten their lives. Such efforts would aim ultimately to undermine the morale of the dictators' troops and finally to subvert their loyalty and obedience in favour of the democratic movement. Similar strategies could be aimed at the police and civil servants.

The attempt to garner sympathy from and, eventually, induce disobedience among the dictators' forces ought not to be interpreted, however, to mean encouragement of the military forces to make a quick end to the current dictatorship through military action. Such a scenario is not likely to install a working democracy, for (as we have discussed) a coup d'état does little to redress the imbalance of power relations between the populace and the rulers. Therefore, it will be necessary to plan how sympathetic military officers can be brought to understand that neither a military coup nor a civil war against the dictatorship is required or desirable.

Sympathetic officers can play vital roles in the democratic struggle, such as spreading disaffection and noncooperation in the military forces, encouraging deliberate inefficiencies and the quiet ignoring of orders, and supporting the refusal to carry out repression. Military personnel may also offer various modes of positive nonviolent assistance to the democracy movement, including safe passage, information, food, medical supplies, and the like.

The army is one of the most important sources of the power of dictators because it can use its disciplined military units and weaponry directly to attack and to punish the disobedient population. *Defiance strategists should remember that it will be exceptionally difficult, or impossible, to disintegrate the dictatorship if the police, bureaucrats, and military forces remain fully supportive of the dictatorship and obedient in carrying out its commands.* Strategies aimed at subverting the loyalty of the dictators' forces should therefore be given a high priority by democratic strategists.

The democratic forces should remember that disaffection and disobedience among the military forces and police can be highly dangerous for the members of those groups. Soldiers and police could expect severe penalties for any act of disobedience and execution for acts of mutiny. The democratic forces should not ask the soldiers and officers that they immediately mutiny. Instead, where communication is possible, it should be made clear that there are a multitude of relatively safe forms of "disguised disobedience" that they can take initially. For example, police and troops can carry out instructions for repression inefficiently, fail to locate wanted persons, warn resisters of impending repression, arrests, or deportations, and fail to report important information to their superior officers. Disaffected officers in turn can neglect to relay commands for repression down the chain of command. Soldiers may shoot over the heads of demonstrators. Similarly, for their part, civil servants can lose files and instructions, work inefficiently, and become "ill" so that they need to stay home until they "recover."

Shifts in strategy

The political defiance strategists will need constantly to assess how the grand strategy and the specific campaign strategies are being implemented. It is possible, for example, that the struggle may not go as well as expected. In that case it will be necessary to calculate what shifts in strategy might be required. What can be done to increase the movement's strength and regain the initiative? In such a situation, it will be necessary to identify the problem, make a strategic reassessment, possibly shift struggle responsibilities to a different population group, mobilise additional sources of power, and develop alternative courses of action. When that is done, the new plan should be implemented immediately.

Conversely, if the struggle has gone much better than expected and the dictatorship is collapsing earlier than previously calculated, how can the democratic forces capitalise on unexpected gains and move toward paralysing the dictatorship? We will explore this question in the following chapter.

Nine

Disintegrating the Dictatorship

The cumulative effect of well-conducted and successful political defiance campaigns is to strengthen the resistance and to establish and expand areas of the society where the dictatorship faces limits on its effective control. These campaigns also provide important experience in how to refuse cooperation and how to offer political defiance. That experience will be of great assistance when the time comes for non-cooperation and defiance on a mass scale.

As was discussed in Chapter Three, obedience, cooperation, and submission are essential if dictators are to be powerful. Without access to the sources of political power, the dictators' power weakens and finally dissolves. Withdrawal of support is therefore the major required action to disintegrate a dictatorship. It may be useful to review how the sources of power can be affected by political defiance.

Acts of symbolic repudiation and defiance are among the available means to undermine the regime's moral and political *authority* – its legitimacy. The greater the regime's authority, the greater and more reliable is the obedience and cooperation which it will receive. Moral disapproval needs to be expressed in action in order to seriously threaten the existence of the dictatorship. Withdrawal of cooperation and obedience are needed to sever the availability of other sources of the regime's power.

A second important such source of power is human resources, the number and importance of the persons and groups that obey, cooperate with, or assist the rulers. If noncooperation is practiced by large parts of the population, the regime will be in serious trouble. For example, if the civil servants no longer function with their normal efficiency or even stay at home, the administrative apparatus will be gravely affected.

Similarly, if the noncooperating persons and groups include those that have previously supplied specialised *skills and knowledge*, then the dictators will see their capacity to implement their will gravely weakened. Even their ability to make well-informed decisions and develop effective policies may be seriously reduced.

If psychological and ideological influences – called *intangible factors* – that usually induce people to obey and assist the rulers are weakened or reversed, the population will be more inclined to disobey and to noncooperate.

The dictators' access to *material resources* also directly affects their power. With control of financial resources, the economic system, property, natural resources, transportation, and means of communication in the hands of actual or potential opponents of the regime, another major source of their power is vulnerable or removed. Strikes, boycotts, and increasing autonomy in the economy, communications, and transportation will weaken the regime.

As previously discussed, the dictators' ability to threaten or apply *sanctions* – punishments against the restive, disobedient, and noncooperative sections of the population – is a central source of the power of dictators. This source of power can be weakened in two ways. First, if the population is prepared, as in a war, to risk serious consequences as the price of defiance, the effectiveness of the available sanctions will be drastically reduced (that is, the dictators' repression will not secure the desired submission). Second, if the police and the military forces themselves become disaffected, they may on an individual or mass basis evade or outright defy orders to arrest, beat, or shoot resisters. If the dictators can no longer rely on the police and military forces to carry out repression, the dictatorship is gravely threatened.

In summary, success against an entrenched dictatorship requires that noncooperation and defiance reduce and remove the sources of the regime's power. Without constant replenishment of the necessary sources of power the dictatorship will weaken and finally disintegrate. Competent strategic planning of political defiance against dictatorships therefore needs to target the dictators' most important sources of power.

Escalating freedom

Combined with political defiance during the phase of selective resistance, the growth of autonomous social, economic, cultural, and political institutions progressively expands the "democratic space" of the society and shrinks the control of the dictatorship. As the civil institutions of the society become stronger *vis-à-vis* the dictatorship, then, whatever the dictators may wish, the population is incrementally building an independent society outside of their control. If and when the dictatorship intervenes to halt this "escalating freedom," nonviolent struggle can be applied in defence of this newly won space and the dictatorship will be faced with yet another "front" in the struggle.

In time, this combination of resistance and institution building can lead to *de facto* freedom, making the collapse of the dictatorship and the formal installation of a democratic system undeniable because the power relationships within the society have been fundamentally altered.

Poland in the 1970s and 1980s provides a clear example of the progressive reclaiming of a society's functions and institutions by the resistance. The Catholic church had been persecuted but never brought under full Communist control. In 1976 certain intellectuals and workers formed small groups such as K.O.R. (Workers Defence Committee) to advance their political ideas. The organisation of the Solidarity trade union with its power to wield effective strikes forced its own legalisation in 1980. Peasants, students, and many other groups also formed their own independent organisations. When the Communists realised that these groups had changed the power realities, Solidarity was again banned and the Communists resorted to military rule.

Even under martial law, with many imprisonments and harsh persecution, the new independent institutions of the society continued to function. For example, dozens of illegal newspapers and magazines continued to be published. Illegal publishing houses annually issued hundreds of books, while well-known writers boycotted Communist publications and government publishing houses. Similar activities continued in other parts of the society.

Under the Jaruselski military regime, the military-Communist government was at one point described as bouncing around on the top of the society. The officials still occupied government offices and buildings. The regime could still strike down into the society, with punishments, arrests, imprisonment, seizure of printing presses, and the like. The dictatorship, however, could not control the society. From that point, it was only a matter of time until the society was able to bring down the regime completely.

Even while a dictatorship still occupies government positions it is sometimes possible to organise a democratic "parallel government." This would increasingly operate as a rival government to which loyalty, compliance, and cooperation are given by the population and the society's institutions. The dictatorship would then consequently, on an increasing basis, be deprived of these characteristics of government. Eventually, the democratic parallel government may fully replace the dictatorial regime as part of the transition to a democratic system. In due course then a constitution would be adopted and elections held as part of the transition.

Disintegrating the dictatorship

While the institutional transformation of the society is taking place, the defiance and noncooperation movement may escalate. Strategists of the democratic forces should contemplate early that there will come a time when the democratic forces can move beyond selective resistance and launch mass defiance. In most cases, time will be required for creating, building, or expanding resistance capacities, and the development of mass defiance may occur only after several years. During this interim period campaigns of selective resistance should be launched with increasingly important political objectives. Larger parts of the population at all levels of the society should become involved. Given determined and disciplined political defiance during this escalation of activities, the internal weaknesses of the dictatorship are likely to become increasingly obvious.

The combination of strong political defiance and the building of independent institutions is likely in time to produce widespread international attention favourable to the democratic forces. It may also produce international diplomatic condemnations, boycotts, and embargoes in support of the democratic forces (as it did for Poland).

Strategists should be aware that in some situations the collapse of the dictatorship may occur extremely rapidly, as in East Germany in 1989. This can happen when the sources of power are massively severed as a result of the whole population's revulsion against the dictatorship. This pattern is not usual, however, and it is better to plan for a long-term struggle (but to be prepared for a short one).

During the course of the liberation struggle, victories, even on limited issues, should be celebrated. Those who have earned the victory should be recognised. Celebrations with vigilance should also help to keep up the morale needed for future stages of the struggle.

Handling success responsibly

Planners of the grand strategy should calculate in advance the possible and preferred ways in which a successful struggle might best be concluded in order to prevent the rise of a new dictatorship and to ensure the gradual establishment of a durable democratic system.

The democrats should calculate how the transition from the dictatorship to the interim government shall be handled at the end of the struggle. It is desirable at that time to establish quickly a new functioning government. However, it must not be merely the old one with new personnel. It is necessary to calculate what sections of the old governmental structure (as the political police) are to be completely abolished because of their inherent anti-democratic character and which sections retained to be subjected to later democratisation efforts. A complete governmental void could open the way to chaos or a new dictatorship.

Thought should be given in advance to determine what is to be the policy toward high officials of the dictatorship when its power disintegrates. For example, are the dictators to be brought to trial in a court? Are they to be permitted to leave the country permanently? What other options may there be that are consistent with political defiance, the need for reconstructing the country, and building a democracy following the victory? A blood bath must be avoided which could have drastic consequences on the possibility of a future democratic system.

Specific plans for the transition to democracy should be ready for application when the dictatorship is weakening or collapses. Such plans will help to prevent another group from seizing state power through a coup d'état. Plans for the institution of democratic constitutional government with full political and personal liberties will also be required. The changes won at a great price should not be lost through lack of planning.

When confronted with the increasingly empowered population and the growth of independent democratic groups and institutions – both of which the dictatorship is unable to control – the dictators will find that their whole venture is unravelling. Massive shut-downs of the society, general strikes, mass stay-at-homes, defiant marches, or other activities will increasingly undermine the dictators' own organisation and related institutions. As a consequence of such defiance and noncooperation, executed wisely and with mass participation over time, the dictators would become powerless and the democratic defenders would, without violence, triumph. The dictatorship would disintegrate before the defiant population.

Not every such effort will succeed, especially not easily, and rarely quickly. It should be remembered that as many military wars are lost as are won. However, political defiance offers a real possibility of victory. As stated earlier, that possibility can be greatly increased through the development of a wise grand strategy, careful strategic planning, hard work, and disciplined courageous struggle.

Ten

Groundwork for Durable Democracy

The disintegration of the dictatorship is of course a cause for major celebration. People who have suffered for so long and struggled at great price merit a time of joy, relaxation, and recognition. They should feel proud of themselves and of all who struggled with them to win political freedom. Not all will have lived to see this day. The living and the dead will be remembered as heroes who helped to shape the history of freedom in their country.

Unfortunately, this is not a time for a reduction in vigilance. Even in the event of a successful disintegration of the dictatorship by political defiance, careful precautions must be taken to prevent the rise of a new oppressive regime out of the confusion following the collapse of the old one. The leaders of the pro-democracy forces should have prepared in advance for an orderly transition to a democracy. The dictatorial structures will need to be dismantled. The constitutional and legal bases and standards of behavior of a durable democracy will need to be built.

No one should believe that with the downfall of the dictatorship an ideal society will immediately appear. The disintegration of the dictatorship simply provides the beginning point, under conditions of enhanced freedom, for long-term efforts to improve the society and meet human needs more adequately. Serious political, economic, and social problems will continue for years, requiring the cooperation of many people and groups in seeking their resolution. The new political system should provide the opportunities for people with varying outlooks and favoured measures to continue constructive work and policy development to deal with problems in the future.

Threats of a new dictatorship

Aristotle warned long ago that "... tyranny can also change into tyranny ..."[14] There is ample historical evidence from France (the Jacobins and Napoleon), Russia (the Bolsheviks), Iran (the Ayatollah), Burma (SLORC), and elsewhere that the collapse of an oppressive regime will be seen by some persons and groups as merely the opportunity for them to step in as the new masters. Their motives may vary, but the results are often approximately the same. The new dictatorship may even be more cruel and total in its control than the old one.

Even before the collapse of the dictatorship, members of the old regime may attempt to cut short the defiance struggle for democracy by staging a coup d'état designed to preempt victory by the popular resistance. It may claim to oust the dictatorship, but in fact seek only to impose a new refurbished model of the old one.

Blocking coups

There are ways in which coups against newly liberated societies can be defeated. Advance knowledge of that defence capacity may at times be sufficient to deter the attempt. Preparation can produce prevention.

Immediately after a coup is started, the putschists require legitimacy, that is, acceptance of their moral and political right to rule. The first basic principle of anti-coup defence is therefore to deny legitimacy to the putschists.

The putschists also require that the civilian leaders and population be supportive, confused, or just passive. The putschists require the cooperation of specialists and advisors, bureaucrats and civil servants, administrators and judges in order to consolidate their control over the affected society. The putschists also require that the multitude of people who operate the political system, the society's institutions, the economy, the police, and the military forces will passively submit and carry out their usual functions as modified by the putschists' orders and policies.

The second basic principle of anti-coup defence is to resist the putschists with noncooperation and defiance. The needed cooperation and assistance must be denied. Essentially the same means of struggle that was used against the dictatorship can be used against the new threat, but applied immediately. If both legitimacy and cooperation are denied, the coup may die of political starvation and the chance to build a democratic society restored.

Constitution drafting

The new democratic system will require a constitution that establishes the desired framework of the democratic government. The constitution should set the purposes of government, limits on governmental powers, the means and timing of elections by which governmental officials and legislators will be chosen, the inherent rights of the people, and the relation of the national government to other lower levels of government.

Within the central government, if it is to remain democratic, a clear division of authority should be established between the legislative, executive, and judicial branches of government. Strong restrictions should be included on activities of the police, intelligence services, and military forces to prohibit any legal political interference. In the interests of preserving the democratic system and impeding dictatorial trends and measures, the constitution should preferably be one that establishes a federal system with significant prerogatives reserved for the regional, state, and local levels of government. In some situations the Swiss system of cantons might be considered in which relatively small areas retain major prerogatives, while remaining a part of the whole country.

If a constitution with many of these features existed earlier in the newly liberated country's history, it may be wise simply to restore it to operation, amending it as deemed necessary and desirable. If a suitable older constitution is not present, it may be necessary to operate with an interim constitution. Otherwise, a new constitution will need to be prepared. Preparing a new constitution will take considerable time and thought. Popular participation in this process is desirable and required for ratification of a new text or amendments. One should be very cautious about including in the constitution promises that later might prove impossible to implement or provisions that would require a highly centralised government, for both can facilitate a new dictatorship.

The wording of the constitution should be easily understood by the majority of the population. A constitution should not be so complex or ambiguous that only lawyers or other elites can claim to understand it.

A democratic defence policy

The liberated country may also face foreign threats for which a defence capacity would be required. The country might also be threatened by foreign attempts to establish economic, political, or military domination.

In the interests of maintaining internal democracy, serious consideration should be given to applying the basic principles of political defiance to the needs of national defence.[15] By placing resistance capacity directly in the hands of the citizenry, newly liberated countries could avoid the need to establish a strong military capacity which could itself threaten democracy or require vast economic resources much needed for other purposes.

It must be remembered that some groups will ignore any constitutional provision in their aim to establish themselves as new dictators. Therefore, a permanent role will exist for the population to apply political defiance and noncooperation against would-be dictators and to preserve democratic structures, rights, and procedures.

A meritorious responsibility

The effect of nonviolent struggle is not only to weaken and remove the dictators but also to empower the oppressed. This technique enables people who formerly felt themselves to be only pawns or victims to wield power directly in order to gain by their own efforts greater freedom and justice. This experience of struggle has important psychological consequences, contributing to increased self-esteem and self-confidence among the formerly powerless.

One important long-term beneficial consequence of the use of nonviolent struggle for establishing democratic government is that the society will be more capable of dealing with continuing and future problems. These might include future governmental abuse and corruption, maltreatment of any group, economic injustices, and limitations on the democratic qualities of the political system. The population experienced in the use of political defiance is less likely to be vulnerable to future dictatorships.

After liberation, familiarity with nonviolent struggle will provide ways to defend democracy, civil liberties, minority rights, and prerogatives of regional, state, and local governments and nongovernmental institutions. Such means also provide ways by which people and groups can express extreme dissent peacefully on issues seen as so important that opposition groups have sometimes resorted to terrorism or guerrilla warfare.

The thoughts in this examination of political defiance or nonviolent struggle are intended to be helpful to all persons and groups who seek to lift dictatorial oppression from their people and to establish a durable democratic system that respects human freedoms and popular action to improve the society.

There are three major conclusions to the ideas sketched here:

• Liberation from dictatorships is possible;

• Very careful thought and strategic planning will be required to achieve it; and

• Vigilance, hard work, and disciplined struggle, often at great cost, will be needed.

The oft quoted phrase "Freedom is not free" is true.

No outside force is coming to give oppressed people the freedom they so much want. People will have to learn how to take that freedom themselves. Easy it cannot be.

If people can grasp what is required for their own liberation, they can chart courses of action which, through much travail, can eventually bring them their freedom. Then, with diligence they can construct a new democratic order and prepare for its defence. Freedom won by struggle of this type can be durable. It can be maintained by a tenacious people committed to its preservation and enrichment.

Book Two

The Anti-Coup

by Gene Sharp & Bruce Jenkins

The Anti-Coup

Supporters of political democracy, human rights, and social justice have good reasons to be alarmed about coups d'état. These abrupt seizures of the state apparatus have occurred with great frequency in recent decades. Coups have overthrown established constitutional democratic systems of government, halted movements toward greater democracy, and have imposed brutal and oppressive regimes. Coups d'état are one of the main ways in which new dictatorships are established. Coups may also precipitate civil wars and international crises. Coups remain a major unsolved defence problem.

A coup d'état[17] is a rapid seizure of physical and political control of the state apparatus by illegal action of a conspiratorial group backed by the threat or use of violence. The members of the previous government are deposed against their will. Initially the coup group rapidly occupies the centres of command, decision-making, and administration, replacing the previous chief executive and top officials with persons (military or civilian) of their choice. Eventually they gain control of the whole state apparatus. Successful coups are usually completed quickly, at most within forty-eight hours.

Coups d'état have taken place in dozens of countries in nearly every region of the world in recent decades, including in Thailand, Burma, the Philippines, Brazil, Czechoslovakia, Ghana, Liberia, Chile, Fiji, Greece, Libya, Laos, Guatemala, Argentina, Grenada, Poland, and the Soviet Union.

Coups have been very widespread in Africa in the post-colonial independent countries. The first of these was a military coup which ousted Kwame Nkrumah as President of Ghana in 1966. There were five coups in Thailand between 1951 and 1976, making the growth of democracy difficult. In Libya Muammar Khadaffi took power as a result of a 1969 military coup. The Allende government in Chile was deposed by a military coup in 1973. The 1964 military coup in Brazil brought in a repressive military regime that ruled for years. In Guatemala the 1982 coup was followed by another coup which eventually placed retired General Rios Mott in charge. The 1981 declaration of emergency and installation of General Jarulzelski as president in Poland to repress the Solidarity independent labour union, as well as the failed hard-line coup attempt in the Soviet Union in August 1991, are among the best known examples in recent decades. Coups and coup attempts continue.

Some writers have commented that coups d'état – not elections – "have been the most frequent means for changing governments" and that for postcolonial Africa "the military coup has, in effect, become the institutionalised method for changing governments ..."[18]

It has been suggested that coups are now occurring with less frequency than previously, but also that this decline may be short-lived and that even when a coup has been avoided for many years a country may remain vulnerable.[19]

Massive efforts and sums of money are regularly devoted to prepare to resist foreign aggression. Yet, virtually nothing is done to prepare societies to deal with the defence problem of coups d'état, despite their frequency in world politics. Serious consideration of anti-coup defence is long overdue.

How coups operate

Seizure of the actual political machinery of command and administration will often begin by action against top personnel of the previous government, and seizure of government buildings and offices, military and police headquarters, and control centres for communications and transportation. Coups normally operate very quickly, often within a few hours, and therefore secret conspiratorial planning is important.

Coups are most often conducted by a critical part of the military forces, acting alone or in alliance with political cliques, intelligence organisations (domestic or foreign), or police forces. Sometimes coups have been executive usurpations: an established head of state (president or prime minister, for example), falsely claiming an emergency, acts to suspend constitutional government and establish a dictatorship.[20] Sometimes coups have been led by a dictatorial political party, with or without its own paramilitary forces. Coups may also be initiated by a section of the ruling elite backed by other groups. If the coup is to succeed it is important that non-participants in the coup be supportive, remain passive, or be made ineffective. Because of its minority and conspiratorial nature, a coup is the opposite of a mass popular revolution (although putschists may call their action a "revolution").

The group initiating the coup usually intends to use the power of the section of the state which it already controls (or over which it expects at first to gain control) against the other sections in order to gain complete control of the state. Often the other sections readily capitulate. They may do this in face of perceived overwhelming forces supporting the coup. They may also capitulate because they do not strongly support the established government, have active sympathy for the putschists, or feel helpless, not knowing what else they can do.

The usurpers normally intend to maintain order and to keep the bureaucracy, civil service, military forces, local government, and police intact (at least for the time being), but to bring them under their command. (The new government imposed by a military coup may be fully military, partially military, or fully civilian in personnel.) The combined power of the state under the usurpers can then if necessary be applied against the rest of the society to extend and consolidate the control of the whole country.

When are coups likely to occur?

In some countries an internal coup is unthinkable, as in Norway and Switzerland, for example. Some conditions tend to impede coups. Where democratic constitutional procedures exist, are respected, and provide for peaceful institutionalised means to resolve internal conflicts, to change governments, and to hold government officials accountable, a coup d'état will be less likely. If the groups capable of conducting a coup – as the army – believe in democratic processes and respect the limits that have been placed on their authority, they are unlikely to attempt a coup. They may instead exert self-restraint, believing that it would be wrong to stage a coup.

The social structure of the society is also influential in determining whether a coup d'état is likely to happen. Where the civil, non-state, institutions of the society are strong and democratically controlled, and military institutions and anti-democratic political parties are in comparison weaker, a coup is not likely to occur.

Where the society works together in relative harmony a coup is not likely. That situation, however, is rare and is not required to prevent a coup. If the internal problems are at least of limited severity and can be dealt with by institutionalised and other peaceful procedures, a coup is less likely. Or, if acute conflicts are present but are conducted nonviolently instead of by internal violence, the stage will not be set for a coup by a group that promises to end internal violence and to restore law and order. Where politicians seek to serve the society and avoid corruption, one "justification" for a coup will be removed.

On the other hand, when those conditions are not present, the society may be vulnerable to coups. The roots of democratic political systems may be shallow or eroded. The government may be seen as illegitimate, and there may be widespread dissatisfaction with its performance. Perhaps it may be charged with incompetence, corruption, or indecisiveness in times of crisis. Confidence in the capacity of democratic procedures to remedy the situation may be widely lacking, and in some cases there may be no agreed pro-cedures for succession of governments.

The civil non-state institutions of the society – voluntary institutions of many types, political parties, independent educational institutions, religious bodies, trade unions, and many other types – may be weak or nearly non-existent. Also, the general population may lack significant participation in the political system. Consequently, there would be no groups and institutions capable of opposing a seizure of the state apparatus.

The society may have very serious internal problems associated with violence. Serious social unrest, acute economic problems, sharp political conflicts, or internal violence and assassinations may make the major parts of the society willing to accept a new strong government which promises to act to "restore order" and to end the crisis.

Unfavourable economic conditions, interacting with political factors, may make a society vulnerable to coups, and it has been argued that lack of diversification in exports and excessive dependency on a variable international market for exports can create conditions in which a coup is likely.[21]

At times, individuals, powerful groups, a dictatorial party, or a military clique may simply lust for power and domination – with or without the guise of noble objectives.[22]

Such conditions do not necessarily produce a coup, however. Even when conditions for a coup may be favourable and the potential putschists lack self-restraint, they may not make the attempt because it would likely fail. This propensity to failure may derive from several sources. Important sections of the military personnel, the police, and the civil servants, as well as lower levels of government, may be viewed as unsupportive of a coup and likely to resist the attempt. The independent institutions of the society may be inclined to oppose the coup and are strong enough to act powerfully against it.

The ability of these possible opponents of a coup to act powerfully against a coup attempt can significantly influence the decision of potential coup-makers about whether to make the attempt or not. If a society is likely to resist firmly an attempted takeover, a coup is less likely to occur.

Those who attempt a coup must be able to assume that once they have seized power they will encounter minimal resistance from the bureaucracy and the populace. In societies where the masses are politically mobilised, involved, and powerful, this assumption cannot be made.[23]

Support for coups

The basic prerequisite of a coup is that the putschists' organisational and repressive forces are believed to be more powerful than the other institutions and forces of the society. In short, civil society is weaker than the military forces. Indeed, in many countries, the military forces have been in recent decades expanded to be by far the strongest institution of the whole society. These military forces have often been turned against the very society and population on which their existence has depended and which they were supposed to defend. Such a military coup is more likely if the soldiers are more loyal to their officers than they are to the democratic government.

If the coup is instead an executive usurpation (sometimes called a "self-coup"[24]), it is necessary that the combined governmental civil bodies and military forces assisting the takeover are more powerful than the civil institutions of the society. Instead, the coup may be one conducted by a disciplined political party with its own paramilitary forces. The party's supporters may also at times operate from key ministries in a co-alition government or with support from significant sections of the military and police. To succeed, that party must be more able to act than are other sections of the society which might oppose the takeover. In some situations, agents of a foreign government may assist internal political or military groups in carrying out a coup.

In past coups, supporters of political freedom have often been silent and have passively submitted. This does not mean that when a coup attempt succeeds that the general population favoured it. In many cases the population may be actually opposed, but does not know what to do. A civil war against the military forces and their allies – a war which democrats would certainly lose – has understandably inspired few. Believers in constitutional procedures and social justice have usually not known how else a coup backed by the military forces could be defeated.

Without serious preparations for an anti-coup de-fence, a lasting democratic system is very doubtful in many countries, especially in those with a history of coups. Even in countries that have achieved a relatively democratic political situation, anti-coup measures are important despite public statements of innocent inten-tions by those individuals and groups that are capable of conducting a coup.

Obviously it is better to have prevented coup attempts from occurring than it is to have to defend against them. One important issue therefore is how coups can be prevented and blocked.

In many constitutional democracies it has been assumed that if the constitution and the laws prohibit coups d'état, then the democracy is safe. That is demonstrably not true, as too many countries have discovered to their peril. Democracies with constitutional provisions or laws against attempts to seize control of the state by coups have themselves been victims of coups. Such legal prohibitions should exist, but many times they have failed to block coups. Coups are in fact always conducted by groups which are quite willing to violate constitutional and legal barriers to their intended actions. This does not mean that such constitutional and legal provisions are not useful, but that they are insufficient. Means of enforcing them are clearly needed.

Persons and groups willing to push aside or murder executive officials in order to install themselves as rulers find no problem in violating existing constitutional or legal barriers to their action. Military groups determined to "save the nation" or to establish their own dominance will not be seriously impeded by a legal barrier. Disciplined political parties that see themselves to be the saviors of the people and the makers of a future ideal society may respect no barriers to their taking state power in order to implement their mission.

Efforts to remove justifiable grievances in the society are also needed, but they too are insufficient. Such grievances may genuinely motivate potential putschists or may be merely excuses for a coup which is attempted for less honourable motives.

International condemnation and sanctions are also unlikely to deter determined putschists.[25] It is naïve to expect that international influences will be able to prevent, or unseat, an internal takeover. At best they may support a strong indigenous capacity to block attempted usurpations. At other times, certain international influences may support the coup, or even be a main force in its instigation, as for example has the United States government been in several cases.

Obviously, then, something more is required: strong barriers to coups d'état. This essay will argue that these barriers can be erected within the country by a prepared anti-coup defence policy. This policy would not only have the potential of defeating coups. It could also serve as a potential deterrent to these attacks, rooted in the capacity for effective defence.

Because coups have so often been successful, populations are often unlikely to think that effective anti-coup barriers can be erected. The confusion and sense of powerlessness which often accompany coups have been aggravated by the population's absence of planning, preparations, and training to block coups.

When the coup is commonly backed by the military forces, the supposed defenders of the society, against which there can be no military power applied, the anguish and despair of the population increases.

Coups have been defeated

The problem of how to block coups d'état would seem insoluble, except for the important fact that sometimes coups have been defeated. Despite often disadvantageous conditions, civilians have at times been able to block illegal seizures of state power. These cases have been remarkable.

Sometimes coups fail because noncooperation and defiance break the intended link between physical control of government facilities, and the political control of the state. Civil servants, bureaucrats, military groupings, and other state employees at times steadfastly refused to cooperate with putschists, denying control of the state apparatus. Coups have also been imperiled by severance of the link between control of the central state machinery and control of the society – including independent social institutions, local governments, and the population as a whole. Putschists have often narrowly assumed that dominance of state structures equals political and social control. However, without the submission of all these sections of the society the coup leadership cannot become a lasting government.

The defeat of the attempted hard-line takeover

in the former Soviet Union in August 1991 is one relatively recent case of mass noncooperation against a coup. Prominent earlier cases of successful anti-coup defence occurred in Germany in 1920 against the Kapp Putsch (which threatened the new Weimar Republic) and in France in 1961 against the Algiers generals' revolt (which aimed to keep Algeria French by ousting the de Gaulle-Debré government). In these three cases, and a few others, the coups were blocked by internal nonviolent resistance. Only occasionally, as during the 1991 coup in the Soviet Union, has serious supportive international diplomatic and economic action been threatened or taken.

Germany 1920 [26]

On 12 March 1920, unofficial *Freikorps* units of ex-soldiers and civilians occupied Berlin in a coup against the Weimar Republic organised by Dr. Wolfgang Kapp and Lieutenant-General Walter von Lüttwitz. The coup aimed to establish an authoritarian regime of "experts." The small German army remained "neutral."

The legal democratic government under President Friedrich Ebert fled. Though not well prepared, the coup might well have succeeded had there been no resistance. The legal government proclaimed that all citizens should obey only it, and that the provinces should refuse all cooperation with the Kapp group. After a workers' strike against the coup broke out in

Berlin, a proclamation calling for a general strike was issued under the names of President Ebert and Social Democratic ministers – though without their official approval.

The Kappists were quickly met with large-scale noncooperation by civil servants and conservative government bureaucrats, among others. Qualified persons refused to accept ministerial posts in the new regime. Kappist repression was harsh, and some strikers were shot to death. However, the strength of the noncooperation grew, and a general strike paralysed Berlin. The *Reichsbank* refused funds to the usurpers. On March 17 the Berlin Security Police demanded Kapp's resignation. He fled to Sweden the same day, many of his aides left Berlin in civilian clothes, and Lüttwitz resigned. The Freikorps then marched out of Berlin, killing and wounding protesting civilians as they did so.

The coup was defeated by the combined action of workers, civil servants, bureaucrats, and the general population who had refused the popular and administrative cooperation that the usurpers required. The Weimar Republic survived to face other grave internal problems. The financial costs of the resistance to the attempted coup were modest, and an estimated several hundred persons had been killed and others were wounded by the Kappists.

French President Charles de Gaulle in early April indicated that he was abandoning the attempt to keep Algeria French. In response, on the night of 21-22 April rebelling French military units in Algeria seized control of the capital city of Algiers and nearby key points. However, the coup there could only succeed by replacing the legal government in Paris.

On 23 April the political parties and trade unions in France held mass meetings and called for a one-hour general strike. That night de Gaulle broadcast a speech, heard also in Algeria, urging people to defy and disobey the rebels, ordering the use of "all means" to bring them down. "I forbid every Frenchman, and in the first place every soldier, to carry out any of their orders." Prime Minister Debré warned of an airborne attack from Algiers. However, instead of ordering military action, he called upon the general population to act: "As soon as the sirens sound, go there [to the airports] by foot or by car, to convince the mistaken soldiers of their huge error."

Copies of de Gaulle's speech were duplicated and widely distributed by the population and loyal French soldiers in Algeria. De Gaulle later declared: "From then on, the revolt met with a passive resistance on the spot which became hourly more explicit."

On 24 April ten million workers took part in the symbolic general strike. At airfields, people prepared vehicles to be placed on runways to block the landing of planes. A financial and shipping blockade was imposed on Algeria.

Loyal French troops in Algeria acted to undermine the rebels. Two-thirds of the transport planes and many fighter jets were flown out of Algeria, while other pilots blocked airfields or pretended mechanical failures. Army soldiers simply stayed in their barracks. There were many cases of deliberate inefficiency, with orders and files "lost" and communication and transportation delayed. Civil servants hid documents and withdrew.

On 25 April de Gaulle broadcast an order to loyal troops to fire at the rebels, but there was no need. The coup had already been fatally undermined. The rebel leaders resolved to call off the attempted coup, and during the night of 25-26 April the parachute regiment that had originally seized Algiers withdrew from the city.

There were a few casualties, probably three killed and several wounded in Algeria and Paris. The attack on the de Gaulle government had been defeated by defiance and dissolution.

The Soviet Union 1991 [28]

On 18 August 1991 in an effort to block the radical decentralisation of power in the Soviet Union, a group of hard-line Soviet officials detained Soviet President Mikhail Gorbachev and demanded that he turn over all executive powers to his vice-president. Gorbachev refused.

The self-declared "State Committee for the State of Emergency" – composed of, among others, the Soviet vice-president, prime minister, defence minister, chairman of the KGB, and interior minister – declared a six-month "state of emergency." Opposition newspapers were banned, political parties suspended (except the Communist Party), and demonstrations forbidden. The junta's first decree asserted the primacy of the Soviet constitution over those of the republics and mandated adherence to all orders of the Emergency Committee.

It appeared that the junta had the entire military forces of the Soviet Union at their disposal. Armoured divisions and paratroops were deployed throughout Moscow. In the Baltics, pro-coup forces seized telephone, radio and television facilities and blockaded key ports. Armoured assault units outside Leningrad began to move on the city.

In Moscow, tens of thousands of people gathered spontaneously in the streets to denounce the coup. In a dramatic show of defiance, Russian Federation President Boris Yeltsin climbed upon a hostile tank and denounced the putschists' action as a "rightist, re-actionary, anti-constitutional coup." Yeltsin proclaimed "all decisions and instructions of this committee to be unlawful" and appealed to citizens to rebuff the putschists and for servicemen not to take part in the coup. Yeltsin concluded with an appeal for a "universal unlimited strike." Later that day Yeltsin ordered army and KGB personnel within the Russian republic to obey him, not the putschists.

Thousands gathered in front of the Russian "White House" (parliament building) to protect it from attack. Barricades were erected; trolley buses and automobiles blocked the streets. Although the call for a general strike went largely unheeded, miners in the Kuzbass coal fields and near Sverdlosk did strike.

The putschists decreed a special state of emergency in Moscow because of "rallies, street marches, demonstrations and instances of instigation to riots." On the second night of the coup, resistance organisers pasted leaflets throughout the city's subway system calling for a mass demonstration in front of the "White House" the following day.

In Leningrad, 200,000 people rallied in response to Mayor Anatoly Sobchak's call for "the broadest constitutional resistance" to the coup. Tens of thousands in Moldavia blocked the streets to keep Soviet troops at bay. Leaders of the Ukraine and Kazakhstan denounced the coup. A large rally in Minsk called for mass civil disobedience. Lithuanian President Landsbergis appealed to citizens to surround the parliament building in Vilnius for protection from attack. Emergency sessions of the parliaments of Latvia and Estonia declared full independence from the Soviet Union.

In Moscow, banned opposition newspapers secretly printed *The Common Paper* which called on citizens to resist. A donated radio transmitter allowed the Russian government to broadcast resistance information across the nation through local relay stations. The banned independent radio station "Echo Moscow" continued to broadcast, carrying live speeches from an emergency session of the Russian parliament. Although prohibited, Russian Television technicians put their news programs on videotape and distributed them to twenty cities around the Soviet Union.

Officials in the state controlled media refused cooperation with the putschists. The defiant speeches of Yeltsin and Sobchak were aired on the nightly news program which the Emergency Committee's KGB censor chose not to block. Afterwards, the First Deputy Chairman of Soviet Television, Valentin Lazutkin, received a call from Interior Minister Pugo: "You have disobeyed two orders ... You have given instructions to the people on where to go and what to do. You will answer for this." Defiant crowds swelled in front of the White House that night to protect the Russian government.

Concerted efforts were made to undermine the loyalty of the putschists' forces. Leaflets and food were distributed to soldiers.

Citizens pleaded with tank crews to switch sides. Yeltsin urged discipline: "Don't provoke the military. The military has become a weapon in the hands of the putschists. Therefore we should also support the military and maintain order and discipline in contact with them."

In several cases, entire military units deserted the putschists. Ten tanks in front of the White House turned their turrets away from the parliament building, pledging to help defend it against attack. Mutinies against the putschists were reported at the Leningrad Naval Base and at a paratrooper training academy. Units in the Far East refused to support the junta. In the Russian republic, local interior ministry police and KGB units declared loyalty to Yeltsin. Defence Minister Yasov ordered the Tula division to withdraw from its positions near the White House because of the troops' uncertain loyalty. Interior Minister Pugo disbanded the Moscow police out of fear of disloyalty to the putschists.

In the afternoon of the second day of the coup, the putschists attempted to put together a new assault team to attack the Russian White House. Army paratroops and Interior ministry forces were to surround the White House, clearing the way for an attack by the elite KGB Alpha Group. The head of the Army's paratroops and the commander of the Soviet Air Force, however, refused to take part in the attack. Hours before the planned attack, the commander of the KGB Alpha Group stated that his forces would not take part. "There will be no attack. I won't go against the people."

The following morning, the Defence Board of the Soviet Union voted to withdraw the troops from Moscow. Members of the Emergency Committee were subsequently arrested (one committed suicide).

President Gorbachev returned to power. Casualties were low – a total of five people were reported killed during the coup attempt. The coup had been defeated. Mass public defiance and disobedience in the military thwarted the hard-liners' attempt to return to authoritarian rule.

These three cases of successful resistance – Germany in 1920, France in 1961, and Russia in 1991 – establish that successful defence against coups is possible. Certainly there are other cases in which similar resistance did not succeed, but the existence of successes establishes that under at least some conditions coups can be defeated.

Anti-coup defence

Attention to how coups d'état work and how they can be defeated teaches us much. Together they show that there is no need to be passive and helpless in face of these blows against freedom and justice. Defence can be waged by the attacked society itself.

The basic point of this essay is that a defence policy against coups d'état is possible. The essence of such a defence policy is twofold: (1) that those who attack the constitutional system and intend to replace the elected government by a regime of their own choosing must be denied all legitimacy – they have no moral or political right to become the government, and (2) they must be denied all *cooperation* – no one in the government or in the population should assist or obey them in any way.

In a coup d'état, the seizure of government buildings, transportation and communication centres, and key geographical points is not done for its own sake. Rather, the purpose of those seizures is to control the state apparatus, and hence the country as a whole. The putschists must secure that broad control if the coup is to be successful.

However, the seizure of such points does not by itself give the putschists the control they seek over the government and the society. They will not initially control the population, the political, economic, or social organisations, the governmental structures, nor even all of the military forces and the police. Nor will the putschists be in a position immediately to accomplish any possible ideological objectives. After military, or para-military, forces have occupied government buildings and key centres of communication and transportation, a crucial period inevitably follows in which the putschists must establish and consolidate their control. Even in the absence of resistance, that control requires time and effort to achieve. This need to consolidate control – and the time it takes to effect this – makes an effective defence by the society possible.

The putschists require . . .

Immediately after the coup is started, the putschists require legitimacy, that is, acceptance of their moral and political right, or authority, to rule. Endorsements by moral and religious leaders, respected political personages, and in some cases royalty or past officials, will help them to gain that acceptance.

The putschists require that their control of the state apparatus be accepted by the persons and institutions in whom moral and legitimate political authority resides, whether they are elected officials, unofficial moral leaders, or royalty.

The first basic principle of anti-coup defence is therefore to deny legitimacy to the putschists.

The putschists also require that the civilian leaders and population be supportive, confused, or just passive. The putschists additionally require the cooperation of specialists and advisors, bureaucrats and civil servants, administrators and judges in order to consolidate their control over the society. Journalists and broadcasters, printers and technicians are required to do as they are told. Police, prison officials, and soldiers need to follow orders to make arrests, jail protesters, and execute people as commanded. The putschists also require that a multitude of people who operate the political system, the society's institutions, and the economy will passively submit and carry out their usual functions as modified by the putschists' orders and policies.

In short, in order to consolidate their control putschists require a significant degree of not only legitimacy but also cooperation from the society they intend to rule.

Few or none of these required acts of submission, cooperation, and assistance may be fulfilled, however. They may be jeopardised by repudiation, noncooperation, and defiance. Both the needed legitimacy and the essential cooperation are vulnerable. All these groups and the general population may refuse to do as ordered. The claims to legitimacy can be rejected. The necessary cooperation, obedience, and support can be denied. The consolidation of the putschists' rule can thereby be blocked.

Even moderate opposition may force the attackers to make significant efforts to secure the needed acceptance, cooperation, and support. In a powerful anti-coup defence, the population would prevent the attackers' control of the state apparatus and the country by massive and selective noncooperation, while maintaining their support for the legal government and its call to resist. Strong, determined, and widespread repudiation, noncooperation, and defiance of the coup by the society can block the putschists' objectives and defeat the coup.

The second basic principle of anti-coup defence is to resist the putschists with noncooperation and defiance.

If both legitimacy and cooperation are denied, the putsch may die of political starvation.

Therefore, an anti-coup policy is focused on defence of the society *by the society itself*, not on defence of points of geography, nor even governmental buildings. Geography and buildings are ultimately important to coup leaders only when possession is accompanied by human assistance. Seizure of a school *building*, for example, is of no use to someone seeking to control education without a functioning school including the cooperative pupils, teachers, and administrators. Occupation of a railroad yard gives no control over that piece of transportation if the railroad workers and managers are unwilling to operate the trains according to orders. Control of a parliament building itself gives no control over the actual members of parliament or over the population as a whole which believes in parliamentary government.

Instead of attempting to provide constitutional defence by fighting over buildings and geographical points, people actively defend their institutions, society, and freedoms directly. The priorities of action here are crucial. Insistence on abiding by constitutional procedures, or the maintenance of a free press, for example, are of more direct importance to democracy than possession of a given street intersection or building.

It is of course true that sometimes certain sites and buildings have a special symbolic importance. Civilian defenders may then want to attempt to block the seizure of these sites by placing their bodies between the attackers and the buildings. In 1991, for example, both the Lithuanian parliament building and the Russian "White House" were so protected by people power. One should not generalise too widely from these two cases, however. It should first be noted that a human barricade is not always realistic. Under extreme weather conditions, especially cold, it would be virtually impossible for a human barricade composed of the same individuals to remain in position for very long. Therefore, it is important to remember that anti-coup defence is a defence of the *society*, not of geographical points or buildings, which the putschists are able to seize if they are willing to kill enough people.

If the putschists are uncertain of their own intentions and methods, or if their troops are unwilling to kill many of the defenders, then a defence by human barricades may be successful. However, a serious danger exists in attempts to defend key buildings or other sites by human barricades. If, despite the defenders' efforts, the building is successfully seized by the putschists, the defenders and general population may become unjustifiably demoralised. The defenders may then believe not that only the parliament *building* has been seized, but that *parliament itself* has been destroyed. The defenders and population may believe that the mere physical occupation of the former government headquarters has put the putschists in control.

Extreme care therefore must be used in formulating

strategies and tactics for defence of buildings, so that the defenders and population put the emphasis on defence of the constitutional system and the society's institutions themselves, which can continue whatever the fate of the buildings. The coup leaders cannot control the society's population, institutions, organisations, and government without the submission and cooperation of the population.

The need for preparations

In the three cases reviewed earlier, the defence was improvised, without the advantage of advance planning and preparations. It is surprising how powerful even improvised social action can be. Inevitably, however, such unprepared resistance will be weaker than if careful plans have been laid for defence against such attacks. Confusion, uncertainty as to what to do, ineffectual or counterproductive protests, and costly delays in taking resolute action can all potentially be avoided or reduced significantly by preparations. Conversely, anti-coup defence by an assertive citizenry can be greatly strengthened by specific preparations and guidelines. These guidelines would aim to prepare the citizenry and social institutions to offer collective resistance to any coup. Such preparations would need to include both general guidelines for the defence and also designated responsibilities for members of particular population groups and institutions, such as civil servants, religious leaders, police, journalists, transportation employees, and many others.

Such planning and preparations for anti-coup defence are possible. Whether independent institutions of the society or the government (with cooperation of nongovernmental institutions and organisations) initiate and carry out anti-coup defence will largely be determined by the political situation in the country and the degree of strength and vitality of the society.

The civilian defenders' aims

Under an anti-coup policy, the resisters will aim to:

• Repudiate the putschists as illegitimate with no rightful claim to become the government;

• Make the attacked society unrulable by the attackers;

• Block the imposition of viable government by the putschists;

• Maintain control and self-direction of their own society;

• Make the institutions of the society into omnipresent resistance organisations against a coup;

• Deny to the putschists any additional objectives;

• Make the costs of the attack and attempted domination unacceptable;

• Subvert the reliability and loyalty of the putschists' troops and functionaries and induce them to desert their mutinous officers;

• Encourage dissension and opposition among the putschists' supporters;

• Stimulate international opposition to the coup by diplomatic, economic, and public opinion pressures against the attackers; and

• Achieve international support in communications, finances, food, diplomacy, and other resources.

Resistance: general and organised

Strategies of anti-coup defence might be grouped initially into two broad categories, "general" and "organised."[29] Well in advance of an attack, a number of key points would be selected and identified to the general population as points at which the population should resist, even in the absence of any specific instructions at the time from a leadership group. This type of resistance is called "general resistance." These points might include, for example, efforts to promote the attackers' regime as legitimate, attempts to remake or abolish the elected legislature, measures to remake the courts or impose a new constitution, abridgments of freedom of speech and religion, and efforts to control the society's independent institutions.

Infringement by the attackers on any of these points would be the population's signal to resist. The advance provision of guidelines for general resistance would make wise resistance possible even if the legitimate officials or the initial defence leaders have been arrested or executed. General resistance could also be practiced if the defence leaders' communications with the population have been blocked.

"Organised resistance" differs from general resistance in that the defenders act in accordance with a call or instructions from an anti-coup defence leadership group. This group might consist of members of the legitimate government, officials of the anti-coup defence planning body, or persons selected in some other way. This leadership might, for example, be comprised of representatives of voluntary organisations (educational, civic, labour, religious, political, and others) who have been informally accepted by the society (whether or not their individual identities are publicly known).

Organised resistance would supplement, not replace, general resistance. Often, organised resistance would consist of acts focused on a specific event, or would occur in a specific place or at a designated time. Such resistance may take the form of specific acts of symbolic protests or resistance, of which there are dozens of possible types. Examples would include demonstrations, short strikes, protest marches, protest blackouts, tolling of church bells, defiant flying of national flags (perhaps at half mast), organised letter writing campaigns, the simultaneous reading in religious services of official statements from religious leaders, organised hunger strikes, radio broadcasts from hidden transmitters, and expressions of mourning (either because of brutalities by the attackers or acts of terrorism by one's own people).

Both general resistance and organised resistance are very important in defence struggles against coups d'état. The proportional roles of each will vary with the specific situation.

The importance of strategy

The general technique that has been most effective in anti-coup defence is nonviolent struggle. This avoids fighting the putschists with military weapons, with which the usurpers usually have the advantage. The nonviolent technique also maximises the power of the defenders, vastly increases the possible number of resisters over those able and willing to use violence, and very importantly helps to undermine the morale and reliability of the putschists' soldiers.

The weapons, or methods, of nonviolent struggle –

such as strikes, boycotts, types of political nonco-operation, and mutiny – are not to be applied randomly. These methods should not be selected in accordance with the whims of individuals or in response to minor events, nor should they be applied in a hodgepodge, improvised, or intuitive way. These methods instead will be most effective if they are applied as component parts of a comprehensive, carefully chosen strategy of anti-coup defence.

Attempting to provide defence without formulating a strategy for the struggle is foolhardy. It is also potentially disastrous. One of the major reasons for the failure of some past nonviolent struggles has been the choice of a poor strategy or very often the neglect to develop any strategy at all. Strategy is just as important in nonviolent struggles as it is in military warfare.

There needs to be an overall plan for conducting the entire conflict. This is called a *grand strategy*. Within it, individual strategies need to be formulated to achieve major objectives in the conflict or for use in broad phases of the struggle. A *strategy* is a conception, a general plan, of how best to act in order to achieve one's objectives in a major phase of a conflict, within the framework of the chosen grand strategy. The aim is to use one's resources to maximum advantage to gain one's objective at minimum cost. The chosen strategy determines whether, when, and how to fight.

Within a strategy particular *tactics* – plans for limited actions – and individual *methods* – specific forms of action – are used to implement the strategy.

These actions are more limited in time, scale, or specific issues in order to achieve intended limited objectives.

Strategies for anti-coup defence need to be planned with much thought and extreme care. The strategies need to draw upon the best available resources about strategic principles. They also need to be based on knowledge of nonviolent struggle, the dynamics of coups, the particular conflict situation, and the strengths and weaknesses of both the defending population and the putschists.

Issues of strategy are more varied and complex than indicated here and readers facing strategic decisions are urged to consult more extensive discussions elsewhere.[30]

Anti-coup weapons

The selection of the most suitable methods of action is of vital importance. The initial anti-coup strategy may use certain of the following nonviolent weapons: a stay-at-home by everyone; paralysis of each part of the political system that the putschists attempt to seize; persistent operation of uncontrolled parts of the political system according to pre-attack policies and laws (ignoring decrees and policies of the putschists); filling streets with demonstrators; conversely leaving the streets completely empty; massive subversion of the attackers' troops and functionaries; defiant publication of newspapers and broadcasts by radio and television with news of the attack and resistance; a general strike;

and an economic shutdown (by both workers and managers).

It is important to give primary responsibility in the defence struggle to those methods that directly counter the putschists' initial objectives. These objectives will be primarily related to achieving and consolidating control over the political system and undermining the opposition to the coup. Economic aims are unlikely to be among the putschists' initial objectives. (Economic objectives may be in some cases longer-term aims, such as to keep control of the economic system primarily in the hands of an existing elite or to use the state to take over control or ownership of the economic system.)

Control of the economic system is seldom, if ever, an initial objective of a coup d'état. Therefore, general strikes or economic shut-downs are rarely the most relevant and effective substantive resistance methods in anti-coup action. Applied in short bursts, they can, however, demonstrate the solidity of the will to resist. When applied for an extended period, however, these economic weapons can imperil the capacity of the attacked society to survive its own defence. A general strike, for example, would usually be used only at the very beginning of the anti-coup defence to show the determination of the society to resist the attack, or later in the struggle for some specified but limited purpose, such as to protest extreme brutalities. The general strike or an economic shut-down might also be used when it was thought that a massive and dramatic expression of resistance might strike a *coup de grâce* to the attack.

Much more important initially will be those specific methods that aim directly at the putschists' initial objectives. These would be ones that: (1) show repudiation of the putschists' claims to legitimacy; (2) block their taking control of the political machinery of the state (as by noncooperation of civil servants, police, military forces, lower levels of government, etc.); (3) demonstrate the population's repudiation of the coup and its noncooperation and disobedience against it; (4) block the putschists' efforts to control the means of communication and instead maintain this through various means including print media and radio; and (5) defy the putschists' efforts to neutralise or control the independent institutions of the society.

If the means of defence cited here can be applied massively and effectively to achieve these aims, the coup can only collapse.

Guidelines for general resistance

Guidelines for general resistance against coups can be formulated in advance of any possible coup. Such guidelines would constitute basic elements for an effective anti-coup strategy, instructing the population on how to resist. These could include the following:

• Repudiate the coup and denounce its leaders as illegitimate, meriting only rejection as a government. The denunciation of the putschists as illegitimate should be supported by moral, political, and religious leaders, officials and members in all of the society's institutions (including education, the media, and communications), and national, local, regional, and provincial governments and officials (including heads of state and any royalty). Refuse to give any legitimacy to the putschists by any means, including efforts to negotiate a compromise between them and the legitimate political leaders.

• Regard all decrees and orders from the putschists contradicting established law as illegal, and refuse to obey them.

• Keep all resistance strictly nonviolent in order to make the anti-coup defence the most effective possible. Refuse to be provoked into violent or other imprudent action.

• Refuse and disobey all attempts by the putschists to establish and extend controls over the governmental apparatus and society.

• Noncooperate with the putschists in all ways. This applies to the general population; all experts and technocrats; all leaders of the previous governments and of political parties; all branches of the central or federal government, state, regional, and local governments, including their civil servants and bureaucrats; key occupational and professional groups; all staff of the media and communications; all staff of transportation systems; the police; members and units of the military forces; all judges and employees of the judicial system; the staffs of all financial institutions, both governmental and private; and officers and members of all other institutions of the society.

• Persist in maintaining the normal operations of the society in accordance with the pre-attack constitution, laws, and policies of the legitimate government and the society's independent institutions. This should be continued until and unless the persons are physically removed from their workplaces, offices, and activity centres. Even then as far as possible, continue normal operations from other locations. This applies especially to officials and employees of all branches, departments and levels of government.

• Preserve the functioning of legitimate political and social organisations. Create backup organisations which may need to assume the functions of organisations attacked or closed down by the putschists.

• Refuse to supply vital information to the putschists and their helpers. For example, where it will help, remove road signs, street names, traffic signs, house numbers, etc. to impede the putschists' activities and protect people from arrest.

• Refuse to supply the putschists with needed supplies and equipment, hiding these when appropriate.

• Engage in friendly "creative communication" with the functionaries and troops serving the putschists while continuing resistance. Explain to them the reasons for the defence struggle, affirm the absence of any intended violence against them, seek to undermine their reliability, and try to induce them to be helpful to the defenders. This help might take the forms of deliberate inefficiency in repression, passing information to the defenders, and in extremes to desertion, with soldiers instead joining the defenders in nonviolent struggle for freedom. Attempt to persuade soldiers and functionaries of the need instead to adhere to constitutional and legal procedures.

• Refuse to assist the putschists in disseminating their propaganda.

• Document in writing, sound, and film the putschists' activities and repression. Preserve the documentation and also distribute the information widely to the defenders, internationally and to the putschists' supporters.

Very early in the coup, the defenders would attempt to communicate with and to warn the putschists, their functionaries, and their troops about the population's hostility to the attack. Words and symbolic actions would be used to communicate the will to resist, to show the type of defence that would be waged, and to urge the putschists to withdraw.

Efforts would be made at all phases of the coup to undermine the loyalty of the putschists' individual soldiers and functionaries. This would be relatively easier in anti-coup resistance than in cases of foreign invasions because the soldiers and functionaries would usually speak the same language as the resisters or at least a common language they both understood. If this were not the case, then communication would still be possible in other ways such as the use of translated leaflets and slogans, or linguistically skilled resisters, or through the defenders' behavior and symbols.

The putschists' soldiers would initially be informed that there will be resistance, but that the resistance will be of a special type. In this resistance, the defence would indeed be directed against the attempt to seize control by the coup but would be conducted without harming the soldiers as individuals. If this could be communicated, the soldiers might be more likely to help the defending population in small ways, to avoid brutalities, and to mutiny at a crisis point, than if the troops expected at any moment to be killed by snipers or bombs.

Repeated demonstrations that there is no violent intent or threat toward the individual soldiers, accompanied by clear resistance, are very important. This combination has the greatest chance of increasing the effectiveness of the anti-coup defence. Strong resistance without personal threat or violence may, at least among some soldiers, create or aggravate their morale problems. The problems may be expressed in uncertain loyalties to the putschists, problems of maintaining self-respect while inflicting repression on nonviolent people, and in extremes, disaffection and mutiny.

There can be no guarantee, however, that the putschists' troops will be favorably affected by the nonviolent discipline, especially in the short run. They may still perpetrate brutalities and kill nonviolent resisters. Such tragedies do not, however, mean the failure of the resistance. Instead, given continued, disciplined resistance, brutalities can weaken the putschists and strengthen the defence struggle, as discussed in later sections.

Facing attack: obstruction and communication

Although this anti-coup defence does not work by attacking the putschists' troops militarily, some limited action affecting the troops would be taken even at the first stage of an attack. If identified in time, the deployment of the putschists' troops could be temporarily blocked by obstructionist activities on highways, streets, airports, railroads, and the like. The entry or movement of troops could be delayed by such means as refusal to operate the railroads, blocking highways and airports with many abandoned automobiles and at times on streets and roads by human barricades.

Although such obstructionist activities against the deployment of troops would only be effective briefly, these actions would make clear to the individual soldiers that, whatever they might have been told, they were not welcome as troops of the coup. The people will also urge the soldiers not to believe the coup leaders' propaganda.

As other symbolic actions, the people could wear mourning bands, stage a stay-at-home, conduct a limited general strike, or defy curfews. Such actions would serve two purposes. They would give notice to friend and foe that the coup will be firmly resisted. At the same time the actions would help to build up the people's morale so as to discourage submission and collaboration with the putschists.

These actions, however, would be only a symbolic prelude to the later substantive resistance.

The following symbolic methods might be used to help communicate the population's will to resist to the putschists and their forces: leaflets, letters, radio and television broadcasts, personal conversations, newspapers, posters, banners, diplomatic messages, statements at regional and United Nations meetings, third-party assistance, painted messages and slogans, and special types of demonstrations. These means of communication and warning could be aimed at the attackers' troops, leaders, and current and potential supporters of the coup.

Facing attack: repudiation and rejection

In the first hours, days and weeks after a coup d'état is attempted it is extremely important to take quick and solid action to block the putschists from becoming accepted and from establishing effective control over the state apparatus and the society. An immediate strategy of repudiation and rejection of the putschists and their attack is called for in order to defeat the coup quickly. That strategy would combine repudiation of claims to legitimacy and rejection of cooperation. It would include total or near total noncooperation with the putschists. An early defeat of the coup would make unnecessary a later long-term struggle with an entrenched and therefore much stronger oppressive regime.

Because coup attempts are generally at their weakest point in the first hours and days, it is vital that anti-coup defenders undertake immediate and resolute action against the attackers. The defence must be broad and deep enough in the society to constitute a resolute repudiation of the putschists. The attackers' appeals for "national unity" – meaning supporting them – and to allow them time to prove their good intentions, must be dismissed.

Blocking control by the putschists

Politicians, civil servants, and judges, by ignoring or defying the attackers' illegal orders, would keep the normal machinery of government and the courts out of the putschists' control – as happened in the German resistance to the Kapp Putsch in 1920.

The legislature would neither receive the putschists themselves nor comply with any orders or requests from them. Instead, the legislature might continue sitting and operating under the established constitution, unless or until the members were actually physically removed by the putschists' forces. Or, the legislature could disperse after issuing a call for popular and governmental resistance to the coup. The members of the legislature could then join the population in other aspects of the defence struggle.

Neither the government treasury nor private banks would provide money or credit to the putschists. In 1920, for example, the German Reichsbank refused money to the putschists, declaring that the name of Dr. Kapp, a main coup leader, was not on the list of approved signers for the withdrawal of state funds.

The judiciary would declare the putschists and their helpers an illegal and unconstitutional body.

The courts would continue to operate on the basis of pre-invasion laws and constitution. They would refuse to give moral, legal, and repressive assistance to the attackers, even if they had to close the courts. Order would then be maintained by social pressures, solidarity, and nonviolent sanctions; underground courts and independent arbiters could be used.

The putschists should be met with a blanket refusal by the government bureaucracy and civil servants to carry out their instructions, as occurred in the resistance to the Kapp Putsch. Or, the bureaucrats and civil servants might simply continue the old policies, ignoring the putschists' orders, and disrupting the implementation of new policies.

Police could be most effective when they brazenly defy the putschists, refusing illegitimate instructions while attempting to continue their normal duties. When under extreme duress, they could fake compliance with the putschists' orders but by evasion and deliberate inefficiencies never implement them.

Journalists and printers, refusing to submit to the putschists' censorship, would publish banned newspapers, news-sheets, and other publications in large or many small editions. Broadcasters and technicians would broadcast resistance radio programs from hidden transmitters or from uncontrolled or even foreign territory.

For example, President de Gaulle and Prime Minister Debré broadcast appeals from Paris aimed at French army conscripts and officers involved in the coup in Algeria, calling on them to disobey their rebellious officers.

At the same time, efforts should be made to persuade persons who are participating in the coup, and especially those in lower ranks of the military or other organisations who are being ordered to support the coup, that they should instead refuse to obey orders to carry out illegal activities. Where the dangers to such persons would be great, they might take various types of evasive action or disappear into the general population rather than support the anti-constitutional usurpation.

In some past cases, resisters to government oppression have actively attempted to befriend troops under hostile command to induce them to be mild in their repression or even to join in the democratic resistance. At times such efforts have succeeded. Resisters to coups need to be aware of such options and prepared to apply them.

The cumulative impact of such institutional non-cooperation is to prevent the coup leaders from controlling both the government and the society. By blocking such control, the defenders maintain and even increase their ability to continue long-term resistance, should that be required in case the coup does not collapse quickly.

Putschists facing strong and well-prepared anti-coup defence are likely to be seriously threatened, and therefore may respond with repression. This is certain to be a difficult time for the defenders and the whole population. Arrests, imprisonment, beatings, concentration camps, shootings, executions, for example, may take a heavy toll on the defenders. However, *in themselves* the repressive measures are not decisive unless they invoke fear and submissiveness in the defenders. In fact, the opponents' repression is evidence of the power of the nonviolent struggle, and is no more reason for despair than if, in a regular war, the enemy shoots back, wounding and killing one's own soldiers.

Against an anti-coup defence, repression may be used to crush resistance and also to instill fear. The Chinese saying is "Kill the chicken to scare the monkey." However, as has occurred in numerous struggles, if the resisters and population refuse to be intimidated into submission and passivity, then the repression may fail.

Nonviolent defiance often risks serious casualties, but it seems to produce *far fewer* casualties than when both sides use violence. At the same time, persistence in nonviolent struggle contributes to much greater chance for success than if the resisters had chosen to fight a militarily-prepared opponent with violence.

The putschists may demonstrate grave ruthlessness, such as by killing the head of state and other top political leaders. This brutality may not only be done to frighten the population into acceptance of the coup. Such killings also create clear vacancies in government leadership which the putschists aim to fill themselves. Therefore, an important part of anti-coup preparations is to determine clearly the line of political succession, minimally for several replacements.

The importance of nonviolent discipline

Recognising that violence undermines the dynamics and strength of nonviolent struggle, the putschists may often deliberately seek to provoke the resisters to use violence. Violence and plans to use violence may be falsely attributed to resisters. Repression, particularly brutal repression, may be intended to provoke the resisters into a violent response. At other times, *agents provocateurs* are placed within resistance groups to instigate or even commit acts of violence in order to support the charge that the resisters are using violence. All these provocations to violence must be rebuffed if the defenders are not to undermine their own defence.

This anti-coup defence is based on the technique of nonviolent struggle. A grand strategic requirement of nonviolent struggle is that courageous struggle must be combined with nonviolent discipline.[31] Nothing is to be gained, and a lot can be lost, by the killing of young soldiers who have found themselves in the putschists' army.

The perpetration of violence, especially killings by the resisters, helps to undermine the otherwise non-violent struggle in several ways.

Resistance violence may help unite the putschists' basic supporters and military forces against the anti-coup defenders. In contrast, the main defence strategy regarding such soldiers is to undermine their morale and to induce them to become unreliable and even to mutiny. That aim is made almost impossible to achieve when the soldiers are targets of resistance violence.

Violence by the defenders will be used by the putschists to "justify" overwhelming repression which they wanted to use anyhow.

It will be used to claim that the putschists are saving the country from terrorism or civil war, and are preserving "law and order." Violence by the defenders may also weaken their own side, as people may be less willing to support or employ violence than participate in a fully nonviolent resistance.

Repression of defiant and disciplined nonviolent resisters can at times have the opposite effect to that intended by the repressor. In this situation there is a strong tendency for the violent repression to react against the repressors' own power position. This is the process called "political *jiu-jitsu.*"

Repression against courageous but nonviolent resisters can harm the repressors' power position in several ways. Such repression and the impact of brutalities may at times help to increase the numbers of resisters among the defending population and increase their determination. They may also sow doubts and reservations in the minds of the putschists' troops and other supporters, creating unease, opposition, and finally disaffection and resistance among the attackers' own population, functionaries, and military forces. Heavy repression against the nonviolent defenders may also arouse stronger international opposition to the coup and mobilise international opinion and diplomatic and economic action against the putschists.

This process of political jiu-jitsu is a great help when it occurs. However, the strategy of the anti-coup defence should not depend upon it. The strategy should instead concentrate primarily on the repudiation of the putschists' legitimacy and defy their attempts to gain control through massive noncooperation and political defiance.

In summary, maintenance of *nonviolent* resistant behavior by the anti-coup defenders is likely to contribute to: (1) winning sympathy and support, (2) reducing casualties, (3) inducing disaffection and mutiny of the opponents' troops, (4) attracting maximum participation in the nonviolent struggle, and (5) winning wider support. Nonviolent discipline is a key factor in achieving these aims.

Only occasionally, as against the August 1991 Soviet coup, as well as in opposition to the September 1991 coup in Haiti, has serious supportive international diplomatic and economic action been threatened or taken against coups d'état. However, as the case in Haiti of international sanctions to restore President Aristide suggests, successful defence against coups by largely international action may not be effective. Instead, successful defence primarily depends on noncooperation and defiance within the attacked country.

Sometimes, however, international support can be influential in assisting anti-coup struggles. Governments could refuse diplomatic recognition of the putschists and declare a prohibition on economic aid, as the United States and other countries did in reaction to the 1991 Soviet coup attempt. Such governments and societies could also provide technical and economic assistance, publishing, radio, and television services, and telecommunications support to the civilian defenders. Such measures could be planned in advance.

The nonviolent and defiant character of this type of anti-coup defence may stimulate much international publicity and sympathy. At times political sympathy may lead to diplomatic and international economic pressures against the putschists. In the defeat of the August 1991 attempted coup d'état in the Soviet

Union, the internal actions – especially reluctance of soldiers within the military to obey the putschists' orders – seem to have been much more important. However, the diplomatic pressures and threats of international economic action seem to have been a significant supplementary factor. This case illustrates that under certain conditions international pressures can further weaken the putschists and strengthen the cause of the civilian defenders. However, there should be no romanticism that international public opinion or even international diplomatic and economic pressure can defeat a coup without determined and strong defence by the attacked society itself.

Shifts in strategy during the struggle

Shifts in strategy by the civilian defenders may be required at certain points to counter new objectives of the attackers, to correct for exposed weaknesses or unexpected strengths among the defenders, and in order to maximise the impact of the defenders' resistance – based on denying legitimacy and refusing cooperation.

The coup leaders may soon discover that they are confronted by a comprehensive fighting force of the general population, organised through its social institutions. The putschists may at some point realise that they are unable to bring the society under their control, and that the defence is strong enough to force them to call off the whole venture. If this does not occur, the defenders must intensify their efforts to undermine the attackers' regime.

Where the putschists' control has already weakened significantly, or appears likely to do so shortly, it may be time for another intense application of the strategy of repudiation and rejection. This may prove, however, to be simply another phase of the conflict followed instead by a strategy of concentrating resistance only at especially important issues. Or, the total noncooperation strategy may prove to be a final blow to the coup.

A durable success

Success in anti-coup defence depends on several key factors. These include, among others, the spirit of resistance, the solidarity of the defending population, the strength of the defending society, the ability of the people to maintain resistance and nonviolent discipline, the strengths and weaknesses of the putschists, the choice of the putschists' strategy of attack, and the wisdom of the defence strategies.

Victory with this anti-coup defence will come only to those who have developed it into a refined and powerful political tool operating with a wise strategy. As with military conflict, genuine power capacity and defence strength are required in this type of defence.

Defeat of the constitutional defenders is always possible, just as defeat occurs in traditional war. However, there are strong signs that a determined people will have strong chances of achieving success with such an anti-coup defence, and that with fewer casualties and less destruction than would accompany a military struggle.

In case of need for long-term defence

If the anti-coup defence is not successful within days or a few weeks, a new strategic situation will have been created. The putschists will have probably succeeded in establishing a modicum of legitimacy, acceptance, cooperation, and control. The conflict will then have been changed from a short-term anti-coup defence to a longer-term struggle against an established dictatorship. For that rather different conflict situation only some suggestive lines of resistance can be outlined here.[32]

In that resistance a strategy of total noncooperation with the new government would probably not be viable because of the need of the society to survive a longer-term struggle. Instead, a policy of concentrating resistance at various key points would be needed until a resulting change in the balance of forces merited an application of more widespread or total noncooperation in order to bring final success.

A longer-term defence strategy against an established dictatorship needs to focus on two main objectives. First, the attackers must be prevented from obtaining any other major objectives beyond the dictatorship itself. If the dictators seek other forms of domination, as economic, ideological, or political, then liberation plans need to concentrate on blocking these. This produces a strategy of "selective resistance," sometimes called "resistance at key points."

Under a strategy of selective resistance, people in various professions and occupations might resist only on crucial issues. For example, the police, while attempting to keep criminal elements from taking advantage of the situation, might selectively refuse to locate and arrest democratic resisters, perhaps warning people of impending arrests and repressive actions. Teachers would refuse to introduce the regime's propaganda into the schools. Workers and managers would use strikes, delays, and obstructionism to impede exploitation of the country. Clergymen would continue to preach about the duty to refuse to help the dictators.

The second main objective of long-term defence is the protection of the autonomy of the society's institutions. When quick success of the anti-coup resistance has not occurred, the new dictators may attempt to control and silence various institutions of the society. These attempts would especially focus on those institutions that have been involved in the earlier defence struggle, such as the courts, schools, unions, cultural groups, professional societies, religious institutions, and the like. If control over such institutions is achieved, the future capacity of the society for resistance will be further weakened. Therefore, the long-term democratic struggle must firmly resist any efforts of the invader to control the society's institutions. Such institutions are not only points of resistance. They are also actual or potential resistance organisations which can act to defend the society from dictators and to restore the legitimate political system.

The strategy of selective resistance is cited here only to show that an initial failure to defeat a coup need not doom the society to long-term dictatorship. However, the main anti-coup defence should aim to block the usurpation fully and quickly, well before the putschists have consolidated their control.

Collapsing the coup

Such a long-term defence against an established dictatorship may not be needed, however. The initial anti-coup defence struggle may well succeed. If the civilian defenders maintain their discipline and persist in their defiance and noncooperation despite repression, and if they involve significant sections of the populace, the putschists' drive to achieve their aims can be frustrated and finally blocked.

The resistance of a prepared people and their institutions may finally prove to be too much for the coup leaders. Their objectives may be denied to them. Their effort to establish control over the society may have failed. The coup attempt may have merely placed the putschists in a political hornets' nest. The numbers of determined, noncooperating, and disobedient defenders may steadily grow. It may become clear that the defiant defenders are headed for success, a victory enhanced with new vitality and durability.

Great care will then be needed in the transition back to the constitutional system, especially if former political leaders have been killed by the putschists. Where possible, constitutionally selected leaders should be restored to their positions and the previous constitution and laws applied, to be amended in the future where appropriate. Steps should be taken as soon as possible to begin correcting any legitimate problems and grievances that led dissatisfied people to support the coup. The society and government will also do well to consider carefully how the government's democratic qualities can be improved.

Deterring coups d'état

A well-prepared defence capacity against coups d'état can constitute a formidable deterrence against would-be putschists. When a society is known to have a well-prepared anti-coup defence, would-be usurpers anticipating at best a very hard struggle and at worst an ignominious defeat, may well never even attempt a coup.

If would-be putschists or even current government leaders know that if they do not abide by the constitutional limits on their authority, the democratic will of the society will be enforced by political defiance and noncooperation, then they may well decide to stay within their appropriate constitutional roles.

This deterrence capacity is completely dependent upon a credible capacity to wage effective resistance against coups d'état. Hence, the only way to prepare deterrence of internal usurpations is to lay the groundwork for strong noncooperation and defiance against such attacks.

As in military defence, no deterrence capacity is guaranteed to succeed. Attacks may nevertheless occur. If a coup is attempted despite extensive preparations for resistance, then this type of defence could defeat it effectively and potentially very quickly, and restore constitutional government, without the risk of civil war.

Promoting an anti-coup defence

An early step toward this policy will need to be dissemination throughout the society of the concept of anti-coup defence and exploration of the forms of resistance that are most powerful in defending against usurpations. An informational and educational program can be initiated by individuals and organisations even while the concept is quite new. Articles, newspaper reports, public meetings, discussion groups, radio, television, panel discussions, speakers for various organisations, pamphlets, and books, are among the means of communication and education which can be used. Familiarity with the concept that coups can be successfully resisted through noncooperation and defiance is a prerequisite for the needed careful consideration and active support from the major civil institutions of the society and for organised preparations for such defence.

Obviously, consideration, adoption, and implementation of this anti-coup defence should not expect support from cliques intent on potentially conducting a coup. However, the anti-coup policy will be strengthened if it receives "transpartisan" consideration, support, and participation. A transpartisan approach would aim to incorporate people and groups with differing convictions and political opinions in support of the development, adoption, and implementation of the anti-coup policy. Given such varied and wide-ranging consideration the support of most of the population for the anti-coup policy will likely be stronger and more united.

Adopting an anti-coup defence

There are three main ways in which a strong anti-coup defence capacity can be adopted: (1) through widespread dissemination, throughout all levels of the society, of knowledge and understanding of the grand strategy and broad forms of anti-coup resistance, as just discussed; (2) through the organisation of the institutions of civil society so that they are prepared to confront and resist such an attack; and (3) through constitutional and legal changes and organisational efforts within the governmental structure so that it will not be at the disposal of putschists. Ideally, all three of these ways should be applied in sequence or some combination, depending on what is possible or most feasible at the time in the particular situation. However, it is possible to begin the process of education and consideration without certainty as to what will be the final manner of adoption and implementation.

Preparations by the civil institutions

Despite the vulnerability of many democratic governments, not all political leaders will see the desirability and feasibility of preparing for anti-coup defence. A capacity for defence against coups d'état is nevertheless important, and needs to be developed. Where the government for whatever reason does not take the initiative in adopting an anti-coup defence policy and preparing for it, the way is open in societies with any degree of civil liberties for the society itself to take action. In these cases there is a very important role for direct preparations for anti-coup defence by the civil institutions themselves.

In many situations the basic concept of anti-coup defence and the principles of resistance can be disseminated, and preparations for it may be initiated by the civil institutions of the society, independently of governmental involvement.

These preparations would not mean, of course, that

everyone thinks that the current government is the best possible or that it has no serious limitations or problems. The view would simply be that the regime that might be imposed by possible putschists would most likely be significantly worse. Blocking the imposition through a coup of a more autocratic and repressive government would then be a prerequisite to making needed improvements in the political system and society.

Often the targeted current government may suffer from blatant inadequacies, such as widespread corruption, or social disruption, such as a "breakdown of law and order." Putschists may sincerely or falsely claim that their coup is necessary to correct these situations. That claim may give them significant popular support. Nevertheless, defence is needed against those coups.

The new regime may not end corruption, and the claim to support "law and order" may be used to impose a new authoritarian or dictatorial regime. The use of a coup to correct such problems represents a dangerous precedent as to how a problem regime should be changed. That coup might in fact take a very different turn, and the next coup might be much more sinister. One of several possible alternative remedies includes carefully focused campaigns by conventional forms of action or narrowly directed nonviolent protests or resistance.

As an anti-democratic technique of political change, coups d'état are intrinsically dangerous even when it is claimed they are intended to correct a serious problem.

In politics, there are often unintended consequences of one's actions, and not all intentions are always made public.

Nongovernmental institutions and organisations can disseminate the essential concept of anti-coup defence widely throughout the society through various means of communication. Those civil bodies can then individually and in cooperation with others initiate and implement an anti-coup defence policy. They may do this by educating their own constituents, making preparations, and undertaking planning as to how their sector of the population and society might most effectively act to help to defeat a future coup. For example, individuals, groups, and institutions working in communications, transportation, government offices, the police, religious life, education, and every major aspect of the society would need to plan how effectively to block control by the putschists.

Strong preparations for anti-coup defence can merge into both education and the organisation within governmental structures even when a national anti-coup defence policy has not been adopted. In some situations organised preparations by the civil institutions might also involve local and regional governments and cooperation with personnel and groups within the national governmental structure.

This type of planning would need to focus to a significant degree on those aspects of the society that would be priority areas of legitimisation and control for the putschists. Among the high priority areas would be control of the governmental apparatus (civil servants, bureaucrats, and the like) and control of the police and members of the military forces. Also highly important would be newspapers, radio, television, telephones, water, energy, and food supplies. Through such initiatives in education, organisation, planning, and preparations, national plans to block future coups could be prepared that are suited to specific national conditions. Such a defence policy could be made powerful even without governmental initiative.

If such institutions are strong and represent the diverse components of the society, it is possible for them to prepare and to conduct a sufficiently powerful anti-coup defence that is able to defeat such an attack even when the government itself has not participated in the organisation of such defence.

Government-initiated preparations

Where the society has a high degree of democracy, or at least the political leaders wish their society to evolve peacefully without abrupt changes by coups d'état, governments may adopt anti-coup defence policies. Legislatures and other parts of the government can establish measures to prepare for effective defence against future coups. These measures might be aided by constitutional, legal, and organisational changes aimed to bar putschists from seizing control of the government and society.

For example, in 1997 Thailand adopted a new constitution that takes a major step in this direction. Its Article 65 states: *A person shall have the right to resist peacefully any act committed for the acquisition of power to rule the country by a means which is not in accordance with the modes provided in this Constitution.*[33]

Obviously, such a constitutional provision is of major significance. However, to be effective it requires the addition of legal provisions for implementing the principle, and also both governmental and non-governmental preparations to make the noncooperation sufficiently powerful so as to be successful.

Where possible, involvement of the government itself in the dissemination of the concept of defence against coups, and in the preparations for a vigourous defence can have significant advantages. The most important advantage would of course be the direct preparation of the governmental machinery to resist a takeover. The bureaucracy, civil service, ministries, administrative departments, police, and military forces could be trained to offer strong resistance. Specific obligations and guidelines for anti-coup resistance would be developed for and by civil servants, media staff, communications operators, police, military forces, and employees of local, regional, and provincial governments. If these components of the state machinery can be kept unusable by putschists, the defence will be more extensive and powerful than if this were not the case. Also, the struggle is likely to be shorter with fewer casualties.

Possible legislation and other plans
to mobilise defence

Governmental preparations may require new legislation and implementation of its provisions. Among the steps that can be taken are these: (For a fuller discussion of governmental preparations, see Appendix One. For a discussion of preparations by civil institutions, see Appendix Two.)

• A constitutional amendment can be adopted that grants citizens the right and responsibility to resist a coup and denies them the right to recognise a coup as being legitimate.

• Legislation can be enacted that obliges all police and military forces to refuse to participate in or assist with a coup.

• Legislation can be enacted that obliges all government employees to refuse cooperation with a coup and obedience to usurpers. In the event of a coup, government employees would be obliged to carry on their work according to established constitutional and legal procedures and policies.

• Legislation can be enacted that obliges all personnel in the fields of communications, media, and transportation to resist censorship by the putschists and to refuse to cooperate with, or communicate orders from, coup leaders.

• Legislation can be enacted that obliges all public and private financial institutions to refuse financial relations with the putschists.

• The constitutional government can communicate in advance of a crisis with all international bodies, organisations, and governments with which it has relations that in the event of a coup, those bodies should maintain recognition of the constitutional government and refuse all relations with the putschists.

• In the event of a coup, individuals and bodies within the constitutional government can appeal to religious and moral leaders to denounce the attack and to impress upon their adherents that they should refuse to cooperate with it.

• The constitutional government can make plans for continuation of leadership in case important government buildings are seized or government officials are imprisoned or executed.

• The legislature can prepare plans for how the constitutional government should resume control of the country once a coup attempt collapses.

• The legislature can appeal to organisations and educational institutions to develop and implement programs to educate citizens on their right and duty to refuse cooperation with an attempted coup.

In all of this planning, it must be made clear that the nature of the anti-coup resistance is nonviolent and that no one is to commit acts of violence against fellow citizens who illegally support the coup. It should also be made clear what the penalties are for individuals who are found guilty of either initiating or cooperating with a coup.

Other types of preparations

In addition to preparation and dissemination of general guidelines for anti-coup resistance, several other types of preparations for defence are possible. For example, training maneuvers could be organised in which imaginary coups would be defied by staged civilian resistance. These maneuvers could take place in residential areas, offices or factories, cities, provinces, and across the whole country.

Technical preparations would also be necessary for this type of defence against coups. Provisions and equipment would be required for communications after the putschists had occupied key centres and seized facilities of established newspapers and radio and television stations. Publishing supplies and broadcasting equipment for underground newspapers, resistance leaflets, and underground radio could be secured and hidden for use in emergencies. Advance arrangements should be made for locating such broadcasting stations, communications centres, or printing plants, in the territory of a friendly supportive country.

Consequences of an anti-coup defence

The objective of this defence policy against coups d'état is to preserve constitutional government by blocking the imposition of viable government by the putschists, by making the attacked society unrulable by the attackers, and by enabling the population to maintain control and self-direction of their society even when under attack. The responsibility for this preservation of constitutional government rests with all members of the society. It is they who can maintain and expand their freedoms and continue to improve their society in accordance with the cherished principles of the nation.

This anti-coup defence policy would have major positive qualities. It is a policy based on people, not bullets and bombs, on human institutions, not military technology. It is a policy that can serve freedom instead of threatening civil war or submitting to a new dictatorship. Adopted and practiced widely internationally, this policy would make a major contribution to removing the coup d'état as a major political problem. This would limit the rise of new dictatorships, reducing the prevalence of tyranny in the world.

This policy is a creative defence based on the power of people even in grave crises to become, and remain, the masters of their own destinies. The consequences of this could be profound.

Appendices
& Notes

The Methods of Nonviolent Action

The Methods of Nonviolent Protest and Persuasion

Formal statements
1. Public speeches
2. Letters of opposition or support
3. Declarations by organisations and institutions
4. Signed public statements
5. Declarations of indictment and intention
6. Group or mass petitions

Communications with a wider audience
7. Slogans, caricatures, and symbols
8. Banners, posters, and displayed communications
9. Leaflets, pamphlets, and books
10. Newspapers and journals
11. Records, radio, and television
12. Skywriting and earthwriting

Group representations
13. Deputations
14. Mock awards
15. Group lobbying
16. Picketing
17. Mock elections

Symbolic public acts
18. Display of flags and symbolic colors
19. Wearing of symbols
20. Prayer and worship
21. Delivering symbolic objects
22. Protest disrobings
23. Destruction of own property
24. Symbolic lights
25. Displays of portraits
26. Paint as protest
27. New signs and names
28. Symbolic sounds
29. Symbolic reclamations
30. Rude gestures

Pressures on individuals
31. "Haunting" officials
32. Taunting officials
33. Fraternisation
34. Vigils

Drama and music
35. Humorous skits and pranks
36. Performance of plays and music
37. Singing

Processions
38. Marches
39. Parades
40. Religious processions

41. Pilgrimages
42. Motorcades

Honouring the dead
43. Political mourning
44. Mock funerals
45. Demonstrative funerals
46. Homage at burial places

Public assemblies
47. Assemblies of protest or support
48. Protest meetings
49. Camouflaged meetings of protest
50. Teach-ins

Withdrawal and renunciation
51. Walk-outs
52. Silence
53. Renouncing honours
54. Turning one's back

The Methods of Social Noncooperation

Ostracism of persons
55. Social boycott
56. Selective social boycott
57. Lysistratic nonaction
58. Excommunication
59. Interdict

Noncooperation with social events, customs, and institutions
60. Suspension of social and sports activities
61. Boycott of social affairs
62. Student strike
63. Social disobedience
64. Withdrawal from social institutions

Withdrawal from the social system
65. Stay-at-home
66. Total personal noncooperation
67. Flight of workers
68. Sanctuary
69. Collective disappearance
70. Protest emigration (*hijrat*)

The Methods of Economic Noncooperation:
1 – Economic Boycotts

Action by consumers
71. Consumers' boycott
72. Nonconsumption of boycotted goods
73. Policy of austerity
74. Rent withholding
75. Refusal to rent
76. National consumers' boycott
77. International consumers' boycott

Action by workers and producers
78. Workmen's boycott
79. Producers' boycott

Action by middlemen
80. Suppliers' and handlers' boycott

Action by owners and management
81. Traders' boycott
82. Refusal to let or sell property
83. Lockout
84. Refusal of industrial assistance
85. Merchants' "general strike"

Action by holders of financial resources
86. Withdrawal of bank deposits
87. Refusal to pay fees, dues, and assessments
88. Refusal to pay debts or interest
89. Severance of funds and credit
90. Revenue refusal
91. Refusal of a government's money

Action by governments
92. Domestic embargo
93. Blacklisting of traders
94. International sellers' embargo
95. International buyers' embargo
96. International trade embargo

The Methods of Economic Noncooperation:
2 – The Strike

Symbolic strikes
97. Protest strike
98. Quickie walkout (lightning strike)

Agricultural strikes
99. Peasant strike
100. Farm workers' strike

Strikes by special groups
101. Refusal of impressed labour
102. Prisoners' strike
103. Craft strike
104. Professional strike

Ordinary industrial strikes
105. Establishment strike
106. Industry strike
107. Sympathetic strike

Restricted strikes
108. Detailed strike
109. Bumper strike
110. Slowdown strike
111. Working-to-rule strike
112. Reporting "sick" (sick-in)
113. Strike by resignation
114. Limited strike
115. Selective strike

Multi-industry strikes
116. Generalised strike
117. General strike

Combinations of strikes and economic closures
118. *Hartal*
119. Economic shutdown

The Methods of Political Noncooperation

Rejection of authority
120. Withholding or withdrawal of allegiance
121. Refusal of public support
122. Literature and speeches advocating resistance

Citizens' noncooperation with government
123. Boycott of legislative bodies
124. Boycott of elections
125. Boycott of government employment and positions
126. Boycott of government departments, agencies and other bodies
127. Withdrawal from government educational institutions
128. Boycott of government-supported organisations
129. Refusal of assistance to enforcement agents
130. Removal of own signs and placemarks
131. Refusal to accept appointed officials
132. Refusal to dissolve existing institutions

Citizens' alternatives to obedience

133. Reluctant and slow compliance
134. Nonobedience in absence of direct supervision
135. Popular nonobedience
136. Disguised disobedience
137. Refusal of an assemblage or meeting to disperse
138. Sitdown
139. Noncooperation with conscription and deportation
140. Hiding, escape and false identities
141. Civil disobedience of "illegitimate" laws

Action by government personnel

142. Selective refusal of assistance by government aides
143. Blocking of lines of command and information
144. Stalling and obstruction
145. General administrative noncooperation
146. Judicial noncooperation
147. Deliberate inefficiency and selective non-cooperation by enforcement agents
148. Mutiny

Domestic governmental action

149. Quasi-legal evasions and delays
150. Noncooperation by constituent governmental units

International governmental action
151. Changes in diplomatic and other representation
152. Delay and cancellation of diplomatic events
153. Withholding of diplomatic recognition
154. Severance of diplomatic relations
155. Withdrawal from international organisations
156. Refusal of membership in international bodies
157. Expulsion from international organisations

The Methods of Nonviolent Intervention

Psychological intervention
158. Self-exposure to the elements
159. The fast
  (A) Fast of moral pressure
  (B) Hunger strike
  (C) Satyagrahic fast
160. Reverse trial
161. Nonviolent harassment

Physical intervention
162. Sit-in
163. Stand-in
164. Ride-in
165. Wade-in
166. Mill-in
167. Pray-in
168. Nonviolent raids

169. Nonviolent air raids
170. Nonviolent invasion
171. Nonviolent interjection
172. Nonviolent obstruction
173. Nonviolent occupation

Social intervention
174. Establishing new social patterns
175. Overloading of facilities
176. Stall-in
177. Speak-in
178. Guerrilla theater
179. Alternative social institutions
180. Alternative communication system

Economic intervention
181. Reverse strike
182. Stay-in strike
183. Nonviolent land seizure
184. Defiance of blockades
185. Politically motivated counterfeiting
186. Preclusive purchasing
187. Seizure of assets
188. Dumping
189. Selective patronage
190. Alternative markets
191. Alternative transportation systems
192. Alternative economic institutions

Political intervention

193. Overloading of administrative systems
194. Disclosing identities of secret agents
195. Seeking imprisonment
196. Civil disobedience of "neutral" laws
197. Work-on without collaboration
198. Dual sovereignty and parallel government

Acknowledgements and Notes
on the History of From Dictatorship to Democracy

I have incurred several debts of gratitude while writing the original edition of this essay. Bruce Jenkins, my Special Assistant in 1993, made an inestimable contribution by his identification of problems in content and presentation. He also made incisive recommendations for more rigourous and clearer presentations of difficult ideas (especially concerning strategy), structural reorganisation, and editorial improvements.

I am also grateful for the editorial assistance of Stephen Coady. Dr. Christopher Kruegler and Robert Helvey offered very important criticisms and advice. Dr. Hazel McFerson and Dr. Patricia Parkman provided information on struggles in Africa and Latin America, respectively. However, the analysis and conclusions contained therein are solely my responsibility.

In recent years special guidelines for translations have been developed, primarily due to Jamila Raqib's guidance and to the lessons learned from earlier years. This has been necessary in order to ensure accuracy in languages in which there has earlier been no established clear terminology for this field.

From Dictatorship to Democracy was written at the request of the late U Tin Maung Win, a prominent exile

Burmese democrat who was then editor of *Khit Pyaing* (The New Era Journal).

The preparation of this text was based over forty years of research and writing on nonviolent struggle, dictatorships, totalitarian systems, resistance movements, political theory, sociological analysis, and other fields.

I could not write an analysis that had a focus only on Burma, as I did not know Burma well. Therefore, I had to write a generic analysis.

The essay was originally published in installments in *Khit Pyaing* in Burmese and English in Bangkok, Thailand in 1993. Afterwards it was issued as a booklet in both languages (1994) and in Burmese again (1996 and 1997). The original booklet editions from Bangkok were issued with the assistance of the Committee for the Restoration of Democracy in Burma.

It was circulated both surreptitiously inside Burma and among exiles and sympathisers elsewhere. This analysis was intended only for use by Burmese democrats and various ethnic groups in Burma that wanted independence from the Burman-dominated central government in Rangoon. (Burmans are the dominant ethnic group in Burma.)

I did not then envisage that the generic focus would make the analysis potentially relevant in any country with an authoritarian or dictatorial government. However, that appears to have been the perception by people who in recent years have sought to translate and distribute it in their languages for their countries.

Several persons have reported that it reads as though it was written for their country.

The SLORC military dictatorship in Rangoon wasted no time in denouncing this publication. Heavy attacks were made in 1995 and 1996, and reportedly continued in later years in newspapers, radio, and television. As late as 2005, persons were sentenced to seven-year prison terms merely for being in possession of the banned publication.

Although no efforts were made to promote the publication for use in other countries, translations and distribution of the publication began to spread on their own. A copy of the English language edition was seen on display in the window of a bookstore in Bangkok by a student from Indonesia, was purchased, and taken back home. There, it was translated into Indonesian, and published in 1997 by a major Indonesian publisher with an introduction by Abdurrahman Wahid. He was then head of Nadhlatul Ulama, the largest Muslim organisation in the world with thirty-five million members, and later President of Indonesia.

During this time, at my office at the Albert Einstein Institution we only had a handful of photocopies from the Bangkok English language booklet. For a few years we had to make copies of it when we had enquiries for which it was relevant. Later, Marek Zelaskiewz, from California, took one of those copies to Belgrade during Milosovic's time and gave it to the organisation Civic Initiatives. They translated it into Serbian and published it. When we visited Serbia after the collapse of the Milosevic regime we were told that the booklet had been quite influential in the opposition movement.

Also important had been the workshop on non-violent struggle that Robert Helvey, a retired US Army colonel, had given in Budapest, Hungary, for about twenty Serbian young people on the nature and potential of nonviolent struggle. Helvey also gave them copies of the complete The Politics of Nonviolent Action. These were the people who became the Otpor organisation that led the nonviolent struggle that brought down Milosevic.

We usually do not know how awareness of this publication has spread from country to country. Its availability on our web site in recent years has been important, but clearly that is not the only factor. Tracing these connections would be a major research project.

From Dictatorship to Democracy is a heavy analysis and is not easy reading. Yet it has been deemed to be important enough for at least twenty-eight translations (as of January 2008) to be prepared, although they required major work and expense.

Translations of this publication in print or on a website include the following languages: *Amharic* (Ethiopia), *Arabic*, *Azeri* (Azerbaijan), *Bahasa Indonesia*, *Belarusian*, *Burmese*, *Chin* (Burma), *Chinese* (simplified and traditional Mandarin), *Dhivehi* (Maldives), *Farsi* (Iran), *French*, *Georgian*, *German*, *Jing Paw* (Burma), *Karen* (Burma), *Khmer* (Cambodia), *Kurdish*, *Kyrgyz* (Kyrgyzstan), *Nepali*, *Pashto* (Afghanistan and Pakistan), *Russian*, *Serbian*, *Spanish*,

Tibetan, Tigrinya (Eritrea), *Ukrainian, Uzbek* (Uzbeki-stan), and *Vietnamese*. Several others are in preparation.

Between 1993 and 2002 there were six translations. Between 2003 and 2008 there have been twenty-two.

The great diversity of the societies and languages into which translations have spread support the provisional conclusion that the persons who initially encounter this document have seen its analysis to be relevant to their society.

JANUARY 2008
ALBERT EINSTEIN INSTITUTION
BOSTON, MASSACHUSETTS

Legislation and Other Governmental Preparations
for Anti-Coup Defence

Important preparations can be made by governments to prevent and defeat coups d'état. These may require new legislation and implementation of its provisions. In all of this legislation and these declarations of responsibilities and duties, it shall be made clear that no one is to commit acts of violence against one's fellow citizens who are acting illegally. The following legal measures and procedures are recommended for this purpose.

1. A constitutional provision should be adopted that no citizen of any status, role, or position in the society whatsoever has the right to accept as the legitimate government any person or group that has conducted a coup d'état.

To the contrary, all citizens without exception have the constitutional duty to deny legitimacy to any group of putschists and to refuse all cooperation with them and all obedience to them. Citizens will persistently continue their usual duties and assist in meeting the human needs of their fellow citizens while defying the putschists.

2. Specific laws should be enacted to establish the legal obligations of all government employees and civil servants, on national, regional and local levels of government, to refuse to assist coups d'état. Their legal obligation would be to persist in conducting their work according to established (pre-coup) constitutional and legal procedures and policies only. They would also be legally bound to refuse all cooperation with and obedience to any group of usurpers. This refusal would be aimed to deny to putschists all administrative support to carry out their illegal orders and objectives.

3. Specific laws should be enacted to implement the new constitutional provision to make it a legal obligation of all members of police forces and all members of the military forces to swear not only allegiance to the constitutional government, but to pledge – perhaps in the induction oath – to refuse to participate in any conspiracy to organise or conduct a coup d'état. In case a coup is then later attempted, it would be the duty of these persons to refuse to obey, serve, or collaborate with any group that has attempted to seize the state apparatus.

The police at all levels and members of the judicial system must be mandated to continue to apply the previously established laws, policies, and procedures only. They must ignore any new policies, edicts, and orders, received or announced, from those who have illegally attempted to seize the state. Specifically, they may warn persons and groups of the likelihood of arrest, and they should refuse to locate and arrest patriotic resisters who are defying the putsch, either by individual actions or by group resistance and demonstrations.

At times this police resistance may be quite open and at other times police may pretend to be obeying the putschists but not actually doing so. For example, they may report that it was impossible for them to locate and arrest wanted persons.

If ordered to disperse street demonstrations, police actions may range from simply being present at the site but not taking repressive measures to joining the demonstrators as resisters themselves. The police must not be allowed to become a tool of repression for the usurpers.

4. In addition to resisting the putschists, police should, wherever feasible, be obligated to actively assist the resistance. For example, it has happened in past resistance movements that police transported supplies of resistance newspapers and other literature in police cars to other parts of the city or region where they were needed.

5. Soldiers and other members of military forces must not allow themselves to become a tool of repression in the service of those who have attempted to replace the constitutional government. Their noncooperation and disobedience may be especially difficult when the coup has been conducted by officers of the military

forces, as compared to a political group which seeks the compliance of the military forces in enforcing their illegal domination on the government and society.

Similarly to the options for police, soldiers in this difficult situation who oppose the coup may take any one of a range of actions, none of which serves the usurpers. They may, for example, be very gentle in facing street demonstrators, or, when ordered to fire at protesters, may shoot above their heads so as not to injure anyone. They may also seek to encourage their military unit to openly defy the usurpers, or, without using their military weapons, soldiers may engage in especially dangerous acts of protest and defiance against the putschists.

Open resistance by both police and military troops is likely to be extremely dangerous as the penalty for disobedience and mutiny is often execution. Consequently, other less obvious ways of denying usurpers obedience and assistance merit investigation and application.

6. Specific laws should be enacted to make it a legal obligation of all persons and organisations working in communications to persist in their loyalty to the constitutional government only. This would mean that in the event of a coup d'état they would be legally bound to refuse to submit to the putschists' attempts to impose censorship, publish announcements and orders from the putschists, and comply with any other illegal orders from the putschists.

In case the regular communications, printing and broadcasting facilities are made unusable for normal activities and for use on behalf of the legitimate government as a result of repressive actions of the putschists, it should be the responsibility of people in those professions, as well as other citizens, to create new means of communication among the population outside the control of the usurpers.

7. All persons and groups working for any level of government should, in the event of a coup, for as long as possible, continue to apply established policies and procedures and ignore any new policies, orders, and instructions issued by the usurpers.

Under likely initial conditions, the government employees can continue this defiance at their usual places of work. If intolerable repression is launched against them there, these persons and groups can go on strike or even disappear. The machinery of government must not be permitted to become a tool of the usurpers for controlling the society as a whole.

8. Specific laws should be enacted to make it a legal obligation of all persons and organisations working in transportation to refuse all orders from the usurpers and to make the transportation system unusable by the putschists and instead to use it to assist the resistance.

9. Specific laws should be enacted to make it a legal obligation of all governmental and private financial

bodies, all banks, business institutions, and other financial institutions, and all labour unions and similar associations, to refuse all financial relations whatsoever with the putschists.

10. Well in advance of a coup attempt, the government should communicate to all governments with which it has diplomatic relations, and to all international organisations, including the United Nations, that those bodies are requested to refuse to conduct any normal political or economic relationships with potential usurpers and instead should recognise the constitutional government only.

11. The legislature and governmental ministries and departments should make various types of contingency plans for the continuation of legitimate leadership in case the putschists occupy government buildings, imprison or execute government officials and representatives, or take similar repressive actions.

12. The legislature should in advance make precise plans as to how constitutional government shall resume full normal operations upon the collapse of the attempted coup. No other group of usurpers shall be permitted undemocratically to impose its own rule during a period of transition. In case of loss of life by previous officials during the coup and defence against it, provisions should be made as to how other persons

may legitimately assume the constitutional positions that have been vacated.

13. The legislature should in advance of an attempted coup urge and support all independent institutions, organisations, associations, and all educational institutions of the country to participate in the education of their members and the general citizenry as to their appropriate patriotic duties to repudiate the usurpers and to practice noncooperation and defiance against any attempted coup d'état.

14. The legislature may also enact legislation to deny participants in a coup any lasting financial gain from their illegal activities. They would also be prohibited from holding any future government employment or positions.

15. The legislature should also consider what other types of punishment should be provided in the law for initiating and cooperating with a coup. These provisions need to take into consideration the need to encourage early supporters of a coup to reverse their action and to join the defence against it.

Preparations
By the Civil Society for Anti-Coup Defence

Coups d'état are less likely to be attempted and more likely to be defeated if the institutions of civil society are prepared and able to resist any attempted seizure of the state.

This defence would be prepared and waged by the nongovernmental organisations and associations, educational institutions, economic organisations, communications and transportation bodies, religious organisations and institutions, and other bodies.

This resistance action by civil society may be waged either in support of planned governmental defence measures, or, in their absence, may be waged independently and directly at the initiative of the citizenry.

In either case, advance preparations for anti-coup resistance by the society's independent institutions are likely to make any coup plotters think twice before attempting such an attack. If they nevertheless attempt a putsch, these preparations would increase the power of the anti-coup defence.

These preparations and resistance can be grouped roughly into five types of activity: (1) public education; (2) media; (3) political organisations; (4) religious institutions; and (5) specific groups and institutions.

1. Public education

The tasks of these nongovernmental bodies would include educating their members and the general citizenry about effective means to reject as illegitimate any usurpers and how to wage widespread noncooperation and defiance of the putschists' efforts to govern. The aim would be to make illegitimate controls and rule impossible.

While all institutions of civil society should participate in these efforts to educate their own members, certain institutions would be especially suitable for reaching the general public. These would include the formal educational system and various branches of the media, such as newspapers, magazines, radio, television, the internet, and the cinema. The political content of such public education measures would include both: (1) the importance of denying legitimacy to any putschists and, (2) the importance of noncooperation and defiance to make it impossible for them to establish and maintain their illegitimate rule. In addition to explicit instructions on how to resist, documentaries and film dramas about cases of earlier anti-coup resistance could be used. Information on consequences in other countries of the failure to resist a coup d'état could also be important.

The public will need to be informed about the characteristics of nonviolent struggle, including its many methods, and the way it operates in conflicts.

At times open street demonstrations may be useful

to communicate opposition to an illegal seizure of the state. However, at other times such action as street marches toward the guns of the putschists' troops may be most unwise. Such action may lead not only to massive casualties but also strike fear into the public, and therefore submission.

Because of these situations, the public must be informed well in advance of the crisis about alternative forms of protest and defiance that are less obviously dangerous but that make popular opposition unmistakably clear. For example, if the mass of the urban population for specified periods simply stays indoors, in their homes, schools, or other buildings, the streets will be largely empty of people, and therefore not be suitable shooting ranges to kill and intimidate resisters. The empty streets will, however, communicate widespread opposition.

2. Media

The members of society's media – journalists, newspaper and magazine editors, radio and television reporters and directors, printing unions, communication aides, and the like – can organise advance resistance against a coup d'état. This would include plans to resist censorship by the putschists, plans to communicate messages from the constitutional government to the general citizenry, and plans to refuse to communicate messages from the putschists to the population.

In addition, media personnel can make advance preparations for communications in case they lose their operational centres or must go into hiding. If the putschists take control of society's media apparatus, printers unions, radio operators, and others can claim mechanical failures and inability to carry out the putschists' instructions. Plans for underground printing presses and secret radio broadcasting capacity can also be developed. Preparations to broadcast from neighbouring countries can be arranged as well.

All of these actions will significantly limit the legitimacy and control that people could give to coup leaders because those leaders will be unable to exercise full control over the information to which the society has access and the defenders will be able to communicate widely among themselves and with the public.

3. Political organisations

Both political parties and nonpartisan organisations devoted to advancing their social, economic, and political agendas should include in their missions efforts at educating their members and the public as to the importance and methods of anti-coup defence. Their prior organisational contacts and networks can also help significantly in communicating guidance about needed resistance and conducting the anti-coup defence.

4. Religious institutions

Religious and moral leaders and groups should urge their believers and supporters to regard a coup as an attack on constitutional democracy that is both immoral and a violation of the codes of behavior by which their adherents and believers should live. Consequently, if such an attack occurs, those religious and moral leaders and groups should urge their believers and supporters to apply their beliefs by refusing to give any legitimacy to the putschists, refusing all cooperation with and obedience to them, and instead by participating actively in the anti-coup defence.

5. Specific groups and institutions

The members and officials of individual groups and institutions in the society could also organise around preventing the putschists from controlling the areas of the society that they operate. For example, members of civil society who work in transportation, economic activities, mass media, communications, religious institutions, and all other major functioning components and services of the society need to prepare and apply noncooperation and defiance to retain their independence from putschists.

It will be highly important for these bodies and institutions to block attempts by the putschists or their supporters to seize internal control of these bodies and institutions. Attackers may also even attempt to destroy these independent groups and institutions and replace them with new institutions controlled by the putschists or their collaborators. Those efforts, too, will need to be defeated.

The citizens and their nongovernmental institutions should launch preparations and in a crisis should initiate actual resistance.

This anti-coup resistance could be in accordance with an advance governmental anti-coup defence plan or, as noted earlier, could be launched independently if no such plan has been prepared.

Those population groups and institutions that operate or control important social, economic, political, or industrial functions, will usually be more skilled in determining what specific forms of noncooperation and defiance may be most effective in keeping that area of the society out of the control of usurpers than the theorists of such resistance. A few examples follow:

• Transportation workers, such as truck drivers, railroad employees, or airline operators are likely to be far more skilled in determining how best to slow or paralyse the transportation system and to keep it out of the hands of the putschists, than staff in a government office. They are also likely to be most skilled in knowing how, despite partial paralysis by resisters or blockages of transportation by putschists, to move food and other important supplies to places where they are most needed.

• In the communications field, as long as cell phones and email systems are still operating, they can be used creatively to help communicate resistance plans, to initiate resistance activities, and to report the status of putschists' controls and resistance struggle. Reserve broadcast equipment that has been hidden away for an emergency can be used for defence purposes even when government offices or previous broadcasting stations have been occupied.

• Civil servants in government offices can continue to function independently, even if their directors have joined the putschists. In addition to open defiance, civil servants can also quietly resist the coup through bureaucratic slowness, misfiling important papers and similar nonprovocative but effective activities that limit the putschists' control.

• Labour unions can defiantly refuse to follow putschists' efforts to direct economic activities and can continue those activities that have been prohibited, whatever the putschist leaders, collaborating administrators, or corporation officials may say.

• Special days that honour persons, events, or principles of significance to the nation and to the democratic resisters may be observed even when the putschists ban them and new such days may be instituted to honour events or casualties of the anti-coup resistance.

Notes

From Dictatorship to Democracy

1 The term used in this context was introduced by ROBERT HELVEY. "Political defiance" is nonviolent struggle (protest, noncooperation, and intervention) applied defiantly and actively for political purposes. The term originated in response to the confusion and distortion created by equating nonviolent struggle with pacifism and moral or religious "nonviolence." "Defiance" denotes a deliberate challenge to authority by disobedience, allowing no room for submission. "Political defiance" describes the environment in which the action is employed (political) as well as the objective (political power). The term is used principally to describe action by populations to regain from dictatorships control over governmental institutions by relentlessly attacking their sources of power and deliberately using strategic planning and operations to do so. In this paper, political defiance, nonviolent resistance, and nonviolent struggle will be used interchangeably, although the latter two terms generally refer to struggles with a broader range of objectives (social, economic, psychological, etc.).

2 Freedom House, *Freedom in the World*, freedomhouse.org.

3 Ibid.

4 PATRICK SARSFIELD O'HEGARTY, *A History of Ireland Under the Union, 1880-1922* (London: Methuen, 1952), pp. 490-491.

5 KRISHNALAL SHRIDHARANI, *War Without Violence: A Study of Gandhi's Method and Its Accomplishments* (New York: Harcourt, Brace, 1939, and reprint New York and London: Garland Publishing, 1972), p. 260.

6 ARISTOTLE, *The Politics*, transl. by T. A. SINCLAIR (Harmondsworth, Middlesex, England and Baltimore, Maryland: Penguin Books 1976 [1962]), Book v, Chapter 12, pp. 231 and 232.

7 This story, originally titled *"Rule by Tricks"* is from *Yu-li-zi* by LIU JI (1311-1375) and has been translated by SIDNEY TAI, all rights reserved. YU-LI-ZI is also the pseudonym of LIU JI. The translation was originally published in *Nonviolent Sanctions: News from the Albert Einstein Institution* (Cambridge, Mass.), Vol. IV No. 3 (Winter 1992-1993), p. 3.

8 KARL W. DEUTSCH, *"Cracks in the Monolith,"* in CARL J. FRIEDRICH, ed., *Totalitarianism* (Cambridge, Mass.: Harvard University Press, 1954), pp. 313-314.

9 JOHN AUSTIN, *Lectures on Jurisprudence or the Philosophy of Positive Law* (Fifth edition, revised and edited by ROBERT CAMPBELL, 2 Vol., London: John Murray, 1911 [1861]), Vol. I, p. 296.

10 NICCOLO MACHIAVELLI, *"The Discourses on the First Ten Books of Livy,"* in *The Discourses of Niccolo Machiavelli* (London: Routledge and Kegan Paul, 1950), Vol. I, p. 254.

11 See GENE SHARP, *The Politics of Nonviolent Action* (Boston: Porter Sargent, 1973), p. 75 and passim for other historical examples.

12 R. HELVEY, personal communication, 15 August 1993.

13 Recommended full length studies are GENE SHARP, *The Politics of Nonviolent Action* (Boston, Massachusetts: Porter Sargent, 1973) and PETER ACKERMAN AND CHRISTOPHER KRUEGLER, *Strategic Nonviolent Conflict* (Westport, Connecticut: Praeger, 1994). Also see GENE SHARP, *Waging Nonviolent Stuggle: Twentieth Century Practice and Twenty-First Century Potential* (Boston: Porter Sargent, 2005).

14 ARISTOTLE, *The Politics*, Book v, Chapter 12, p. 233.

15 See GENE SHARP, *Civilian-Based Defence: A Post-Military Weapons System* (Princeton, New Jersey: Princeton University Press, 1990).

16 This list, with definitions and historical examples, is taken from GENE SHARP, *The Politics of Nonviolent Action, Part Two, The Methods of Nonviolent Action.*

The Anti-Coup

17 The terms "coup d'état" and "putsch" are used synonymously in this paper.

18 See, for example, ROSEMARY H.T. O'KANE, *The Likelihood of Coups* (Aldershot, England etc.: Avebury, 1987), p. 1; STEVEN R. DAVID, *Defending Third World Regimes from Coups d'Etat* (Lanham, Maryland etc.: University Press of America, 1985), p. 4; J. CRAIG JENKINS AND AUGUSTINE J. KPOSOWA,

"*The Political Origins of African Military Coups: Ethnic Competition, Military Centrality, and the Struggle over the Postcolonial State,*" in *International Studies Quarterly* (1992), Vol. 36, pp. 271-272; STEVEN R. DAVID, *Third World Coups d'Etat and International Security* (Baltimore and London: Johns Hopkins University Press, 1987), pp. 1-2; and STEVEN R. DAVID, "*The Superpower Competition for Influence in the Third World*" in SAMUEL P. HUNTINGTON, ed. *The Strategic Imperative: New Policies For American Security* (Cambridge, Massachusetts: Ballinger, 1982), p. 236. The quotations are respectively from O'KANE, *The Likelihood of Coups*, p. 1 and JENKINS AND KPOSOWA, "*The Political Origins of African Military Coups,*" p. 271.

19 DAVID, *Third World Coups d'Etat and International Security*, p. 153-154, and O'KANE, *The Likelihood of Coups*, p. 135.

20 Genuine emergency actions by an executive that then quickly relinquishes such prerogatives and restores regular constitutional procedures do not constitute coups d'état.

21 See O'KANE, *The Likelihood of Coups*, and for a contrasting view JENKINS AND KPOSOWA, *The Political Origins of African Military Coups.*

22 For a discussion of six types of military coups in third world countries, classified according to motivations and effects, see STEVEN R. DAVID, *Third World Coups d'Etat and International Security* (Baltimore and London: Johns Hopkins University Press, 1987), pp. 13-16.

23 DAVID, *Defending Third World Regimes from Coups d'Etat*, pp. 4-5.

24 From the Spanish *autogolpe*, used to describe cases in Latin America in the early 1990s.

25 This is not to deny that in some circumstances foreign intervention may block or even overturn a coup, especially where an overwhelming military invasion is possible, as in the United States' action in Grenada in 1983. The point is that these cases are exceptions and those means are not dependable. If they are used, they take control of the situation away from the local population.

It could be very easy to underestimate the difficulties that would face the United States, or any future superstate, that adopted a policy of threatening or applying military intervention to block coups d'état generally. STEVEN R. DAVID has pointed to these: "The difficulties inherent in protecting regimes from the consequences of large-scale military threats pale in comparison to the problems involved in devising strategies for the protection of leaderships from indigenously created coups d'état." (DAVID, *The Superpower Competition for Influence in the Third World*, p. 242.)

26 This account is based on WILFRED HARRIS CROOK, *The General Strike* (Chapel Hill, NC: University of North Carolina Press, 1931), pp. 496-527; DONALD GOODSPEED, *The Conspirators* (New York: Viking, 1962, pp. 108-188; ERICH EYCK, *A History of the Weimar Republic* (Cambridge, Massachusetts: Harvard University Press, 1962), Vol. 1, pp. 129-160; KARL ROLOFF (pseud.: KARL EHRLICH). *Den Ikkevoldelige Modstand: den Kvalte Kapp-Kupet*, in K. EHRLICH, N. LINDBERG, AND G. JACOBSEN, editors, *Kamp Uden Vaaben* (Copenhagen: Levin & Munksgaard, Einar Munksgaard, 1937), pp. 194-213; and JOHN WHEELER-BENNETT, *The Nemesis of Power* (New York: St. Martin's

Press, 1953), pp. 63-82. See also GENE SHARP, *The Politics of Nonviolent Action* (Boston: Porter Sargent, 1973), pp. 40-41 and 79-81.

27 This account is based on that of ADAM ROBERTS, "*Civil Resistance to Military Coups*" in *Journal of Peace Research* (Oslo), Vol. XII, no. 1 (1975), pp. 19-36. All quotations are from that source.

28 This account of the August 1991 Soviet coup has been prepared by BRUCE JENKINS, and was previously published in GENE SHARP with the assistance of BRUCE JENKINS, *Self-Reliant Defence Without Bankruptcy or War* (Cambridge, Mass.: Albert Einstein Institution, 1992), pp. 16-19. It was compiled from the following sources: *The Boston Globe*, 20-23 August 1991; *The Economist*, 24-30 August 1991; STUART H. LOORY AND ANN IMSE, *Seven Days That Shook The World, CNN Reports*, (Atlanta: Turner Publishing, Inc. 1991); *Newsweek*, 2 September 1991; *The New Yorker*, 4 November 1991; *The New York Times*, 20-25 August 1991; *Time*, 2 September 1991; *The Washington Post*, 21 August 1991.

29 This clarification was introduced by the late LARS PORSHOLT. See LARS PORSHOLT, "*On the Conduct of Civilian Defense*" in T. K. MAHADEVAN, ADAM ROBERTS, AND GENE SHARP, editors, *Civilian Defense: An Introduction* (New Delhi: Gandhi Peace Foundation, and Bombay: Baratiya Vidya Bhavan, 1967), pp. 145-149.

30 For a good discussion of strategic principles in nonviolent struggle generally, see PETER ACKERMAN AND CHRISTOPHER KRUEGLER, *Strategic Nonviolent Conflict: The Dynamics of People Power in the Twentieth Century* (Westport, Connecticut

and London: Praeger, 1994) See also GENE SHARP, *Waging Nonviolent Struggle: Twentieth Century Practice and Twenty-First Century Potential.* F(Boston: Porter Sargent, 2005).

For more detailed discussions of civilian-based defence strategy, see GENE SHARP, *Civilian-Based Defense: A Post-Military Weapons System* (Princeton, NJ: Princeton University Press, 1990), pp. 89-111; GENE SHARP, *Making Europe Unconquerable: The Potential of Civilian-based Deterrence and Defense* (Cambridge, Mass.: Ballinger Books, 1986), pp. 88-118, (London: Taylor & Francis, 1985), pp. 113-151; and ADAM ROBERTS, *Civilian Defense Strategy* in ADAM ROBERTS, editor, *The Strategy of Civilian Defense* (London: Faber & Faber, 1967); U.S. edition: *Civilian Resistance as a National Defense* (Harrisburg, Pa.: Stackpole Books, 1968) pp. 215-251. Other sources are cited in SHARP, *Making Europe Unconquerable* (Ballinger edition), pp. 160-161, N. 1.

31 See GENE SHARP, *The Politics of Nonviolent Action*, pp. 586-620.

32 See GENE SHARP, *From Dictatorship to Democracy: A Conceptual Framework for Liberation*. Bangkok: Committee for the Restoration of Democracy in Burma, 1993 and Boston: Albert Einstein Institution, 2002.

33 Constitution of the Kingdom of Thailand. A certified correct English translation has been used and can be found online.

www.ingramcontent.com/pod-product-compliance
Lightning Source LLC
Chambersburg PA
CBHW032131020426
42334CB00016B/1123

* 9 7 8 0 6 4 8 5 3 1 5 1 7 *